T0121452

LET GO AND GROW!

Anna Daniel

Balboa Press books may be ordered through booksellers or by contacting:

Balboa Press
A Division of Hay House
1663 Liberty Drive
Bloomington, IN 47403
www.balboapress.com.au
1 (877) 407-4847

Print information available on the last page.

ISBN: 978-1-4525-3032-1 (sc)
ISBN: 978-1-4525-3033-8 (e)

Balboa Press rev. date: 08/06/2015

NEW LIFE!

Yes, believe it is so. New life can only come in when the old one is sorted. Go in my name and heal, teach and enlighten souls that have been hiding in the darkness. My love and light will always be there so claim it and use it for all mankind. Don't speak too much or make of a different attitude from people. They will try anything to trip you up or sending thoughts of disease or disruptions. Stay clear and firm. Only listen to my voice and feel my tender touch upon your shoulder. Just know that I am there and you don't have to worry any more. It's so easy for some to get side-tracked when tired or drained. Let this year and my teaching and growth continue. You never stop learning and never stagnate so keep the water wheel turning and follow through. Also let my love help and to guide you and give you confidence and cheer. It's not always going to be as hard as last year as when you feel stronger you will attract alike. Your new life of work will prove to be rewarding for spirit, and we have organized tools and other needed supplies. Go ahead and love each other.

New Year's blessings TttA

GREETINGS!

Keep on giving away greetings from the source and cheer to all. We only deliver good news and a lot of love. Keep on working and rest in between. Don't concern yourself about to many different ideas from others. That is for them not for you. Let go and stay clear of negativity. Disturbance is everywhere at present time, so keep your guard up and protect yourself three times over. You can keep an eye on the outside world but none can see in. What a good idea you think any way you have that for a long time. The tactics of protection you are aware of and you will learn more as you go along. Keep eyes and ears activated and useful. Rest and relax so we can get through to you better. Enjoy today and smile more, you have reason to. Look for more areas in your life where blessings have been showered on you. How well its going is up to you when you listen in and follow through all is indeed well. So carry on in this New Year to love and laugh. Cheer light and joy for your day.

TttA

PEACE AT ALL COST!

So many tests and so many questions, It's all for a good cause. We are checking you out and testing over and over again. It's the only way we can make sure you can stand up to it all, and don't catch any negativity. So far this morning there have been 4 humans that tried you out and did not get any of your energy. Be compassionate and caring without any involvement. Your new kind of work is coming around the corner, so keep going as you are in the meantime. So many people are trying so hard to rattle you, so think of yourself as a tall pine tree in the storm bending and never in the slightest breaking even a little. See yourself as we see you, forever trying and evolving. Don't be too hard on yourself, but do ask for miracles every day. They do happen and we know best. Keep on surrendering and your faith will grow. Your practical details are in our hands. We will see to it and believe divine timing. When you are close to the divine source you will get instant help always. You are different so your life and actions will be different. That's a good sign all is well and you know deep down that's true.

Love and light from TttA.

TRUST AND FAITH!

Beloved spirit-working for the light that is what we suggest. Only listen to the suggestions and advise. The same as before don't follow any tempting or control. That will only lead you to a downward pattern. To be able to work and commit 100% to the universal spirit is the only way if you want to advance? There are no short cuts to enlightenment and you must follow through and obey the spiritual law. It's been there since time has begun. And it will always be there in your future. Yesterday you felt little sad, for a souls down fall. But it will teach them to be more careful. He has advanced but when pushed he did not recognise the warning signs. Still a lot to release. The New Year is so new and so it will unfold in due course. The ones that need our help the most will be sent to you. Get ready and welcome the wandering one. Start to paint and prepare for the next class, the time for change is getting closer. Gladly embrace new work. The peace and stillness will follow you for ever. Stay close and ask for help if needed.

Blessings and love from TttA

KEEP COMING BACK TO THE SOURCE!

That is the only way you can get recharged and renewed. Get yourself in the best order as possible and keep on refining your life. Wisdom will be given and all the tools that you require. You never have to be short of anything ever again but if it's not appearing at once you would not benefit from that direction now. So wait and don't let it disturb you, only accept it is for the best. Your blueprint is nearly done now. We have not forgotten you and we are noticing every little step ahead. Your trust in us has also increased. That was due to let go of old preprogramed systems, from this life time and others. We have told you that before, but you have not liked it I think nor understood the deeper meaning of it all. Well that's behind you now.

Today you will hear some news. Things are unfolding, whoever comes back to you has another reason now. Listen in and don't get involved emotionally. Beware is still the word, but enjoy the little things in life. Cheer at least one soul every day. But don't use your own mind to decide what or where. Ask us. We are the only ones.

Love and light to all light workers. From TttA

IN THE STILLNESS OF A NEW DAY!

Let the stillness of a new day encourage, support and heal you all. Let the Holy Spirit engulf your very soul and stay and grow there. It's the only way you can advance faster. It's of the most valuable importance that you understand the essence of our teachings. You have gone deeper and understand more, but there is a lot more to learn. As you learn more you will spend more time in withdrawal with us and less time in the world. Also be careful how you see who is entering and who is connecting with you. It's OK to stop and do your daily chores after cleanse and wash. You are now better protected but still be safe and careful. They all think they know you because of past experiences or what they want to see. Let them be for now. They will in due course see when they open their eyes. Still it will be many endings, healings and revelations. You don't yet understand it all, but all of a sudden you will. Steady as she goes. You are your own captain and you are steering across the open seas. Some times with passengers, other times alone. To be able to choose is freedom.

Lots of loving support from TttA

BLESSINGS AND LOVE!

Let this day be a blessed and loving day. There is always a lot to be grateful for. Look around you for opportunities and watch other souls and learn from them, only study from afar. Many people operate from different levels and dimensions. That is not to be copied and all actions have to come from the honest feelings and from the heart. All copy work is for some ones easy way out. They would be wise to go inwards to search what's right for them. Most people are so differently tuned in some way and are more sensitive than others, so tread very carefully when we say so. Some need to talk to others who are looking for peace and silence. All others in between you need to tune in to. So you will be silent until you get the OK. Present situations are being dealt with so leave all that to us. It's complicated at times but you will learn from it all day long. Share the wisdom from us through you and me will give you more.

Lots of love and light from TttA

GOOD NEWS!

Yes my children of light. You will have good news, even if at times you wonder when, so many changes and so many growth patterns, all in different shades of blue. It does not matter about other soul's growth if we don't tell you about some work or message. You still must go ahead with your own progress when it comes down to it at the end of the day. The responsibility is yours to learn and keep on learning. Spend time apart each day and you will understand how important the time really is. Don't go out in public before you have your daily time with us in preparation for the day. Your prayers and love will go with you and out to people you come across after you come back to us and have rest and refill. Follow that pattern and no stagnation will occur. Let go of the last feelings of getting isolated and forgotten, as this is the last thing that you are. So many want to say they don't know how so you tell them and they will respond positively. Keep going on and we are there for you with wisdom, support and love. This year you will have many revelations and visions.

Keep your faith love and trust activated. TttA

JOY AND JEWELS!

How many times have we spoken to you about different kinds of joy? That most of the times can't be bought or acquired for deeds. Joy eternal is something you will find when in contact with us or in many forms feel the joy of just be. Eternal joy lasts forever and will be given when you have reached a certain level of understanding. Jewels are like shimmering lights in the darkness and sparkles in a dim world. Let it remind you about other life times on Earth when you have seen the miracles. Many jewels have been hidden because if found too soon could very likely be misused. The same goes for crystals. It's up to who is holding on to them. Remember they only send out help and healing when the keeper asks for it. As for sending out light it could be send out darkness so look after your Gems so you will get a lot of healing help and happiness. After when in recess you will get reward and reap the benefit from it all. It's all about inflow and outflow. The law about spirit and the universal law. Ponder and think deeply on this truth.

Blessings and love from us all. TttA

PEACE AND JOY!

We all know what's going on Earth. So many changes and so many alterations on all levels. That's for us to deal with. You do only your part to the best of your ability. Let my light shine on you and keep you warm and vital. All the needs and wants of yours will be met. Rest assured all is in hand. The new kind of work of yours will need plenty of practice. Do some every day until everything comes very naturally. We have given you all the tools and all keys of knowledge so it is preparing the way for you and make it all be for the good of all mankind's key to knowledge. This is what we have been preparing you for some time, but you will understand why. Your life will never be the same again. Don't forget to spend time apart with us in meditation. The bigger the task, the more time spent with us. Remember also to talk to people that we have asked you to help. Today will be interesting to put it mildly. Unfolding time and cheers for work well done. Enjoy what's coming your way today!

Blessings and love. TttA

LET THE SPIRIT SOAR!

To activate the spirit to the most highest and in a beneficial way is to grow. Let us activate yours. When you surrender you let us help. It's hard for an independent person to do so but its better and gives more satisfaction. To be able to learn is a privilege. Remember no lesson can be learned if you are not following the rules. It might be a human weakness to alter rules but it will not work if you want to grow. Remember in the past rulers and kings often got bad advice from their so called advisers. All of you should know by now that's not the way. Many would like something new at all times, but it's never new. Only alterations of the same thing. The knowledge has always been there, but hidden until the right person could understand it and use it for a positive advancement. The tools could be used in opposite way when in the wrong hands. It's always a big power struggle on Earth. That will change and the whole energy pattern will alter. It's all about evolving in to a higher realm. Only a few are understanding at the moment but it will be more. Send out light and love to the world to brighten the darkness and greed. Keep on being a light house worker.

Eternal support from TttA

PEACE AT ALL COST!

Harmony is the one of the most important factors in your life. Don't do anything else if there is no harmony and peace. Wrong decisions will make a loss of energy. You know there are a lot of disruptions at present because of the sorting out in the atmosphere. It's been a long time coming so be patient. It's clearing. If you are getting no advice or no positive input you just have to wait. Not ready yet but still we say stay close. This year is a finishing off your subjects and finalising of events and clarifications of situations. Well now you think is it never going to end, well it is. So much going on and so many souls are disturbed. So we have to move slowly. Not to overload anything. Healing is given every 7 nights you are getting better and more balanced. Bear with the situation and don't make any sudden moves in your life, when OK go ahead and enjoy the improvement. Take it as it comes, and don't concern yourself about others too much. Still do what's on your plate and then rest. Courage my friend you will make it.

Blessings and support from TttA

ORDER!

Let nothing stop you to have discipline and order. Too much time is wasted looking for lost and the like. Give a thought to order. It's not a control, only remember to have a system. You all have too many conditions taught from early days, some good and some bad. Have another way to clear with things and people. That's not easy but you can do it, and in the long run you will benefit. Also we need to have a talk about priorities. For some, it will be a lot different from yours but that's because you are on a different path way. You will understand what really is important but it's not easy. When confronted with situations that are new to you. Let us deal with it and we will feed you with what we want you to do. Serious order again. Well that's right, today you have had another reminder about people's weak sides and how easy the temptations creep in. You all get that because you need to experience how strong it can be, and very subtle. Sly faces of negativity. Live and learn, practise and practise. You have plenty of that.

Blessings and love from TttA

ACCEPT THE BLESSINGS THAT COME!

Don't let pride or ego block you from the acceptance of a loveable thought or action. The self has to go otherwise it will also block the nearness of me your guardian master and always the most reliable source and help in all areas. Let today show you how function very well. By the grace of God you all can pass on love light and divine blessings from us. All that lovely energy healing in your garden certainly helps all that comes, so choose to sit there. The little birds and your Goldie are doing their part. Look a little further listen to the bumble bees busy collecting pollen and the rustles of leaves letting you know how much alive they are, and all the life force that comes with them. Don't forget the sound of water. All together you will experience peace serenity and balance. You are so fortunate to be able to be where you are. Look around you and see the colour and beauty of my making. That's for you to nurture and love so all of you would be wise to nurture something or someone.

Lots of cheers and strength from TttA

JOY IN FREEDOM!

Yes my children of light, enjoy the feeling of joy. It is the most beneficial healing roll that's existing on Earth. Remember the old times and the way you used to operate. It will only take you a minute to know what to do. It's so simple when you know how. Feelings of loss an emotions not dealt with is a few of the courses. Look at what is going on and how you feel. Any irritations look closer and detach from it all at once. Quite often it's someone else's garbage. You of all people will know how easy it is picked up and you will were it if not careful. Stay vigilant and always remember to surrender to us for a fast reliable solution. This morning proved it clearly. So much that you have not seen and understood clearly. You are improving, and will keep on doing so like you have been reminded so many times. Back to the universal spirit school. You have the ability to understand so open up your heart spirit and mind more we are protecting you and staying very close for a while. You will see more proof today.

Lots of support thoughts and education from TttA

SLOW MOVEMENT IS BENEFICIAL!

You might think at times that's not moving fast enough but slowly does it. A brick at a time will build a mighty force against attacks and warfare. It does not mean that you are going to have some, but to be ready is always beneficial because you don't see the big picture as yet. It does not mean that you will not understand at the moment if we told you, so trust is a very big part of your lesson. You are beginning to understand how complicated some lives are and how tangled they make it for themselves. The lesson will be repeated time and time again until it's sinking in. You will know how often it will happen best leave all that to us. The same old wisdom as from the past lives. You are recognising the signs better now, as your whole body mind and soul is undergoing a big change so you will be ready for new work, and be prepared for your new chapter to eventuate. Keep going as you are and you will get there. Stop comparing and walk your path.

Lots of loving support and joy from your loving TttA

WISDOM AND JOY!

Do spend a little time to think about wisdom and joy. Joy would be benefit from that. To know is not always enough you most understand when it's wise to act. Get sorted out what's what. The animals do and they use instinct mostly, you know that's OK but spirit knows best. The red tread is not hard to find you are looking too hard at times, so relax and let it all happen. So much of life is not necessary or important. Back to basics is good. Basics for some people are different from others, so remember to ask us for the right questions and versions. Different people have different understandings. Don't copy others too much as you have to find out what's right for you and what's the right level of understanding the person has otherwise it will fall on stony ground. So it's up to you to do much you have to find out what's right, and do your work and prepare the soil. The self has to be completely eliminated and allow the spirit to be in charge. Most think the mind is in charge, but the mind is playing games with most people but it has its purpose. Today's happening will benefit you for the future.

Loving thoughts and actions. TttA

AT LAST!

We meet again late in the afternoon. We have been waiting for you but so many earthly conditions have been taking up your time. You are protected as always but so many think otherwise. Today's connections were of value. New books and new outlets for your books. You have to be strong and brave to be able to handle and deal with all on-going conditions, but you have detailed and deep information on what tools to use which will be given to you as you need them. Watch for media news as it will come with some surprising solutions. Don't query the solutions. We have all that in hand. Just get on with your own clearing and dig deeper still. To be able to understand it all takes lifetimes, and you have been around for many and not always learned your promised lessons. This time it will take away a big chunk of work but you don't really mind. The universal spirit is guiding you and the tools we will supply. Try to relax a bit more as all is said and done but you are listening more. Your friend will understand more after tomorrow. We will be there for him.

Love as always TttA

GLORY TO GOD THE FATHER!

Give all the glory, love and commitment to the father. You all will fully understand how, and much later on Today you will experience a lot of happenings and some answer also will come true. In the heat of the day take a break, and just be. The universal pattern is coming to pass. Once again, your own help and wonderful miracles happen because of faith and love with trust. Wonders will unfold and it's going past thought a lot. Keep up your work and you are coming together nicely. Don't let anyone or anything put you down ever again. You are brave and contagious and persistent. That have helped you through now you can fully understand others similar situations. Somehow you humans trust easier if someone else has had the same experiences. Support and love each other and when you don't know solutions ask and you shall receive. The old truth is very valid and will always be. Cleaning is still going, and there have been a lot of old conditions to deal with.

Amen and blessings from TttA

WISDOM-HOW-WHEN-WHERE!

It's an art and gift from spirit to know how to use wisdom. Which moment and what situations and what are they doing to you, to be able to recognise at once is preferable. In this quite you and what are they doing to which moment and what situation. We know that you want to learn more every day, and you will, but you must take time out to be with us more. So much depends on your balance, peace and harmony. If these three are not there, it will be hard to learn at all, so work on those, You need to look at energies, were they are coming from, In these quiet days you will have the opportunities to study and be an onlooker, early in the morning when stillness is of the most importance so empty out and be ready to receive. Visualise the procedure and follow through. Today you will hear news about a subject you have asked for, so you can fully understand better still be silent and sit before me to learn and get recharged. Trust and love your day.

Blessings and help from TttA

FAITH- LOVE AND TRUST!

Again and again we are reminding you about this three golden grain. You very well know that, but when pressured it becomes an issue, don't let it you only have to surrender and let go of the temporary disbelief. Humans are so made

and pressure, stress or negative thoughts entering your zone throw it out at once. You still are being tested and tried very severely. Many others that you are connected with also are going through their own test, mostly on money, health morals and the justice department. Well, because you live in the world the systems are quite corrupted. You must ask us to sort and clean up, as that is what's stopping you to have progress. The weather and the pets also are very unstable. They are so easy to unsettle and easily get disturbed. The weather is also influencing the people's physical side so extra care is needed but remember it's only temporary. Still we say ask and you will be given. Let us do the protection and give you the wisdom to carry out your tasks and give out what we ask you to do.

Love and courage from TttA

GLAD TIDINGS!

Yes we all could do with just that. It's hard at times to see all the good things it's all around you, and the only thing that's covering things up. It's the material fog. So much down on Earth and too far away from the heavenly input. It's OK to put your feet on the ground. But don't forget to soar up to the spheres. That is what we say and mean when we explain to you about balance. Listen in and one way or the other you and others will get the picture right. It does not matter which way and when as long as you get there. As when you make things, no one will know how long a time it took. They see only the finished product and it's the same for your spiritual growth. The evolvement and the higher thinking and how you dealt with life will change when you are serious about your commitment and open to learning. Back to school is good, you never stop learning, or if you do stagnation will follow and old age. The growth of your nation and the combined gene pool moulds all personalities.

Lots of love, support and spiritual inspiration. TttA

WISDOM!

Again we say to know it all ways is all you have to do. To be wise is the other part that you need to look at. Again, wisdom comes from the spirit that knows what to do and where. Look and wait, ask and then follow, you of all people will fully understand how much is going on, and how many people are involved. The change of energy today was a good thing. You only have to change a little to benefit from the new energies. Your new communication will help you to stay in contact with many. It will also stop the feeling of isolation that you are experiencing so many times. That was for a reason, you did have to learn by being isolated. Some lessons could not have been learned if you are too crowded out. Let bygones be bygones and walk tall whatever occurs. Other people will try to influence you, so stay firm and don't take in more than you have to for any reason. Today is another learning day so learn. No one needs to stagnate. Let it all unfold naturally.

Lots of laughter and joy from TttA

DIVINE SUCCESS!

Well now what is that really? No, not success as you know it. Divine order-discipline surrendering brings success, meaning to advance and understand where how and who in your stage of life. Today you will be noticing another connection. Don't do anything, only observe. So many people are rushing around doing things at all times without thinking about the consequences of it all. Impulsiveness is OK only if spirit prompts it or when it's any danger of any kind, so listen in and follow through, and take time out and ponder. It's good for most people and it will give you time to catch up with your spirit you will discover more keys to your many questions your new cue. Remember to balance it all out so you move in between. Go easy on yourself it's a lot to learn. We will also use it to give you more information faster. Some would like to tell you how when and who to deal with. Ignore them! So once again you have kept your appointment with us, good, and thank you and do keep up your discipline and be patient.

Blessings and love from TttA

MORNING DEW!

Let the dew drops remind you to refresh your spirit every morning. Don't concern yourself about different mornings. It's all for a good cause. So many situations are getting sorted so you feel the alterations and will wonder why. Leave all that to us. Your work is to activate and heal and teach though us. That' a lot of work but time is important, don't let anyone tell you otherwise. They will give up in time when they don't get any results. Enjoy the sunshine and warmth today with your friend from the past. The connection is still quite strong. The other family connection you made will be very interesting, and will sort out what happened a few years ago. The girls did not understand you and anyway they are wandering gypsies with closed imaginations. Always keep an open mind for new ways but let it be known there is nothing new, mostly recycled wisdom. And so people's egos come in to it. Look at real knowledge, as all knowledge comes from the source and the father of all. Blessed be and bless others. We are grateful for the love and light you sent us yesterday. We would like you to carry on that way.

Loving thoughts from us all. TttA

FOCUS ON THE GOLDEN LIGHT!

Lift your eyes up to the higher spheres and make a strong reliable connection. Visualise a lot of pylons going over the country side with electricity going from the source to you all. First you must empty out and then relax ready for new input. Also remember that you are only the middle bridge between souls so pass on knowledge and wisdom and encouragement to all you come across on your travels in different dimensions, sometimes day time or most likely at night when you are visiting us and learn from your teachers. It's quite many now, so your information will be growing and you will need time to-digest it all. Your life is about to change and we have it all in hand. So don't make plans of your own at this point. Little by little the plan will unfold and you will have started to see a pattern in the distance. Clearing and sorting out is still going on, so stay patient and still be vigilant. Your soul level has evolved once more and will keeping doing so. Your physical is also being redone so bear with it and stay where you are. The crystal stage is upon you and it has been so for a long time.

Eternal blessings from us all. TttA.

FEEL FREE-THINK FREE!

Yes my friend that's very important. You know what we are talking about. Never be enslaved by others thoughts, actions and know it all people. Always respect but don't believe, without checking. It might only have been for them at that time, so all those of them need help. Healing needs to be specific for that soul. We have told you that many times but time sometimes is short, but it does not mean any short cut as the principle is quite often the same, because so many people are on different levels of understanding. So back to the saying "you cannot give beef to a baby" When I was on Earth, I spoke in parables for the people to be able to remember and to easily visualise the wisdom from the spheres. I would like to help you with it all. Open minds and hearts to get a wider view on life's confusions and leadership seems to be part of earth problem at present, so back to the strong loveable prayers and light over your planet, as It will in time be peaceful but before that there will be storms and unease and many will object to the power shift. Ride out the storm with our guidance my child of light.

Warmest blessings and love from TttA

SEARCH FOR THE GOLDEN GRAIN!

My beloved, you have searched for many years now, and you have discovered many connections leading to the truth. It's a long journey but a very beneficial one. That's your main purpose this time. With other important parts of your education that might seem to others on a similar path very deep, but it has nothing to do with them. The only thing to understand is that it is between you and the father. To be able to be true to yourself and follow through is more important than you think; otherwise you will have to go back to study harder until you get the picture. All are here to advance and practise wisdom. It would be impossible in one lifetime to do so. The body is only a coat and so treat it very well. It has to fit as a suitable home for the soul. Many times you have lived and worked hard but given nothing to the spirit bank and soul advancement but no life is wasted its learning time and to see that you are going back to school, at times in the same class all for a reason if not a clear picture appears. Ask and you will receive an answer. First empty out, as often there's too much inside so you can't hear or receive anything.

Blessed be, keep going as you are, you are advancing. From TttA

CLEAR GUIDANCE!

Too much of anything will undo good work and you must carry out our wishes if you want to advance. It does not matter how much time it takes. When you are ready it will happen when you are in hurry valuable information could be lost because of stress or other causes. Spirit will move you when you are ready. To listen in and don't get carried away by unimportant issues, Rest and calm will follow when you have discipline, and faith. We are closely watching over you. And we have noticed your hard work. Because you are so highly sensitive you pick up all sorts but you are learning more ways to protect yourself. Trust and don't be afraid. Unchartered waters are not easy to follow. Always remember we have your blue print In hand. Do some work and rest in between. You don't have to think that you haven't tried hard enough, you have. Many old patterns have gone and many new ones have formed. As you feel better so will others that come and visit you in one shape or the other. Stay with what you know and slowly introduced new ideas thoughts and habits. Easy does it.

Love and blessings from TttA

OUR FATHER - YOUR FATHER!

Let's talk for a little wail about place and time you give to the Father. How much thoughts, praise and gratitude do you give to him? He does supply all that we need so don't take it for granted, or forget to give back to him what is a sign of your child spirit & joy, for so much that is given to you. Ask and you will receive but the timing you have been wondering about It will happen when he so decides in another way. You have been told. God is not always there when I want him, but he is usually right on time. We know that you understand, that's because you have not got the full blue print so you can't see where the situation is as sometimes you are too close to it so it will not be in perspective. We have told you and so many others how important that it is to surrender and leave all the making to us and then we can easy give you your part of your work to learn and practise on. As you do you will realise how much there is to learn, but don't forget you have had lifetimes to study and still many more. Stay working as you are and we did send the CM to you yesterday.

More wisdom tomorrow. TttA

WELL NOW—REVELATION TIME!

Let go of more doubt. You do know what has been going on behind the curtain is now becoming quite clear. So many have covered up thoughts, feelings and actions and motives. You only have to ask from now on and do as we say and you will get a better response. Go by your first instruction and detach if you don't get a good feeling from an action person that will happen sometimes as a test. Yesterday it did so you can stand back and look at the event as a learning time. Also take notice who is treating you respectfully or who is arrogant and rude. If in the first instance they are not from the light stay well clear and let us deal with it. Remember when out in public some will stare at you others laugh or becoming puzzled. Wear your new dark glasses and you will be fine. So enjoy your new knowledge, and go ahead with plans. Go along the road of peace harmony and the river of life.

Lots of compassion and joy from us all. TttA

ALERT BUT RELAXED!

Yes you will be wise to do just that. All the alterations are very disturbing to many as a picture you can look at what you are building, and how much is changing but it will be better when it is completed. So bear with it and stay steady and flexible. As it is your antennas are picking up so much more these days. You are becoming so sensitive to all kinds of vibrations, that's a tool for you, your crystal support was another sign that you are on the right track. The smarter the opposition the smarter you must be always the step ahead. We will tell you when it's going to happen so listen in and get ready. We are giving you armour of an invisible force and strength so it can't be discovered by anyone else. Protection from the unseen forces is very important at this time. You only know some of it, only what you need for your work. Too much otherwise to cope with. Focus on today and get more things sorted out. Beware of the smiling faces of the opposition that will try to tempt and entice anyone that could be a subject of energy for them. Subtleness is also a good sign of deception.

Love and strength from TttA

DETACH FROM ALL NEGATIVITY!

Let no one stop or hinder your progress. If not working straight away, leave it to us. We know what causes what, so follow that. Relax and let the sun in and cherish your work. In the future you will be a mighty force for the light and a big thorn their side. That will be a victory for us all. In the meantime carry on as you are. Let today be a learning time, and keep your ears and eyes open and alert. Notice what some people bring as to whether it is appropriate or not. Do keep our appointment and don't delay tasks that are needed to be done. At this point don't ask too much about the future, it's still in the making. If any questions are being asked today, pass it on to us. You had a work night last night. Things got sorted out so go easy today on yourself. Do wait with tasks that are not easy as you soon pick up and become stronger than before. Expect good news and you will get some. Remember the old saying you will be what you think and eat. Look for something nice, funny and joyful and you will have that experience. Move about a little more and you will stir up the energies once again.

Lots of love, support and health. From TttA

FOCUS!

Remember to focus whatever you do, as it will save time and money and unnecessary wasting of energy. Good home and groundwork will also help you to cut down the time of every task. It's all got to do with discipline and you know how big a part it plays in your life. Go ahead and carry out today's tasks and leave complications to us. Don't try to solve the world's problems on your own. Always ask when anything more is needed. It's all got to do with cooperation and communication. Don't expect the other party to say first, or ask for guidance when there is a query. Lots of conditions could have been avoided if only one had spoken up, and got things sorted. Learn from that situation and practise for next situation. That's why we are telling you time after time to ask and pray for the right conditions and the right wisdom to handle what's going on. Bide your time and we will let you know. Remember to check your scent of vibrations. Look ahead and remember once again the past is the past.

Love, faith and trust to all light workers. TttA

STRENGTHEN YOUR BONDS!

Work for today is to firmly cement the bonds to us-the source. We need you as much as you need us. Some would say the need is not right but instead of working it's OK for now. Let go of feeling validated. All people want that but you don't get in by your needs, only when you leave it to us, we give it out. You are trying hard at times and the old life will make you do it, but it will go one day. Stay on line in the meantime and take a day at a time. Remember the picture about the brick. One brick at the time makes a strong fort as well as when you get it dropped on you it will stun you, so you know that the tools can be used both ways. The same goes for your gems, both positive and negative actions, can be taken from every tool so ponder on that today and let the blessings of the day warm and cheer you. Yesterday was another test and you did pass. Practise and practise again and again until it gets right. Don't concern yourself about little things. It will work out for the best.

Love and support from us all. TttA

PEACE AND LOVE TO YOU ALL!

Let the tranquillity of the morning be used as a balm for wounded souls. Beware of people that do not listen or the ones that keep copying, just like a parrot. You need to look at situations in a new light. Too many times you have follow the same pattern and you don't feel that is working anymore, so stop and look at the pattern that was on them at that stage that they were in but now you need a faster clearer way to get to us. Throughout the night you got a lot of information and reassurance. A big new task is in front of you so keep on getting ready and discard any unwanted object or anything that is no longer useful. It's too easy to get used to life as it presents itself but if that the case open your eyes and perhaps ask if you really want that in your new existence, and now much better and easier than before. We will not tell you too much at this stage because you need to digest it all. Keep on going as your pattern is now with small alterations.

Courage and health. TttA

RENEW AND REJOICE!

Let this day be a time do just that. Take the opportunities to use the tools we give you. Don't query when or how just follow through our wisdom. It will turn out OK, but others seem to always wonder about you. They should not waste their time, as so many have tried to change or alter your person one way or the other. It's right at times to just be well meaning souls, but they are not wise enough to know what they are doing. Your own connections overseas do not know anything about you, only what they remember from so many years ago. Maybe it's time to reconnect and stand your ground. All the work you have done for the source for the last 35 years is for the good of all mankind. One day if we so choose we will review what we think is appropriate, In the meantime carry on as we give it to you to do. All tools will be provided. Concern is fine but do remember to do some for yourself. Do only your part and leave all serious work to us. Tonight will be a new experience with new energy coming in to start a new group that will expand in time. We will speak to some searching souls.

Blessings and love from TttA

EMPTY OUT AND YOU WILL RECEIVE!

Remember to do just that. How can anyone receive more where it's no room? Let that be a reminder for you. So many people store experiences. Positive is fine but for goodness sake let all others go. It's human to feel and get emotional but don't let it bother or unease you. Look at the good experiences and remember to thank us. The living wine from the source will sustain you and refill your vessels. Stay firm and be calm, at all costs. You do understand but because of your system you need to ask for reinforcement. To grow a thicker skin is not easy for you, but you are getting there. Balance and patience will also help. Night time is your work time when you come and visit us. Sometimes you come to learn or get healing or just be. Let the day go and you will understand more why things happen. You are too close to what's going on now, but you are doing your best under pressing circumstances. We will reinforce your protection as asked for.

Protection love and cheer from your ever loving team. TttA

GLAD TIDINGS!

Yes we all could do with just that. It's hard at times to see all the good things. It's all around you, and the only thing that is covering things up is the material fog. So much down on Earth and too far away from the heavenly input. It's OK to put your feet on the ground. But don't forget to soar up to the spheres. That is what we say and mean when we explain to you about balance. One way or the other you and others will get the picture right. It does not matter which way and when as long as you get there, as when you make things no one will know how much time it took. They see only the finished product and it's the same for your spiritual growth. The evolvement and the higher thinking and how you dealt with life will change when you are serious about your commitment and open to learning. Back to school is good and you never stop learning or if you do stagnation will follow and old age. The speed of your learning depends of your combination of genes and willingness.

Lots of support, love and spiritual upliftment. TttA

PLEASE UNDERSTAND!

Yes we know you do so many undiscovered truths are coming up from the surface. So you get waylaid a little. Well now I did make you feel better, but at the same time all these old connections are re-entering your life again, unfinished over again, so many lives and so much to learn from it all. We fully understand where you are, and coping quite well. Don't stop now. So much is installed for you, and things to learn and accept. Every age has its own joy and outlook on life. That's fine! Age itself is a number and has got nothing to do with it, only the energy and time you give to yourself and others. We are sending you today so much love and help in all areas. That's needed so you will be able to carry out what's on your plate. It was good that you talked with HD as long as you did as you will know why it's easier. He will understand and develop more in his own good time. Send him light in full measure and we will do the rest. Recharging in your garden will do him good. So many new souls will come this year to your class, and to come and sit and just be. Let that be an encouragement for to you today.

Blessings and love from us all. TttA

AFTERNOON TIME AGAIN!

Well now, you got a different time slot again. We do know but please tell us early as you know we do operate on many different levels. Start to look for a special person that we will send to you for your new work on your #3 book, we have so many other tasks at present time we do operate on many different levels. Your skills with the new tools will be excellent and save some time and money. It will be more interest also for the 2 other books -when the new one is done. Try to organize a special time slot for just that. This morning went well and so will the rest of the day. As well as others that come to you on a Wednesday we will put it to more souls to come so you will have a solid, nice and helpful group. Ask us again and we will be there as prompted. The day will fly and keep you occupied. Take time out and just be looking again as to who is entering your door. They all have a reason for doing so. The lady from B will have a little more info this week. Tell her as she is patiently waiting. Invite her if she chooses to come it will be OK. Clearing ground for future work is at hand.

Blessings and love to you all from TttA.

ORDER!

So much time is wasted when you don't have order. It's understandable in crisis but keep an eye on your life, and what you do with it. Temptation is there many times to get you caught up in other areas, but still do the golden rule and you will get a lot more done. It also means that you will have more time for your spiritual work and relax with rest in between. Slowly at times you are noticing progress here and there so don't give up now. Your choice to do what you are doing. Your lesson to deal and resolve the matter. That is part of your classwork. Don't worry if you don't advance every minute. It's ok to look at the view at your own leisure. When renewed you will look at life afresh. Let that encourage you and also to keep others climbing up the hill of obedience and growth. Your new project needs some consideration but it will give you a lot of new connections. Look, study and digest. The HD combination is useful for understanding in many technical areas. Let it unfold in its own time. This day will also tell a story.

Blessings and light to all TttA

GOOD AFTERNOON!

Well now, a lot of interesting events on the horizon. Carry on as you are and let things be when we say so. Support needed will come. The same as you have been doing for quite a while. It's OK to admit you need help. It will take a little time to come back to where you were, but that's OK. Today's meeting was fine, and later on tonight you will be more informed about different stages of soul levels. You do know but a little reminder now and then to refresh you, and don't concern yourself too much how life will turn out. That's not for you, only deal with what's for you today, so stay cheerful and patient. We have your situation in hand. At times you might not feel so because of unexpected happenings, but rest assured we do have all in hand. Feel calm and protected at all times. You are getting better at the balance. Your family connection tonight is important so be loving and honest. We will help to prepare the ground for you so you will have a little time together. Concerning your other family connection that will take time. There again we will prepare the ground.

Lots of love and light from TttA

CLEANING AND CLEANSING!

Yes my child of light that is exactly what is happening for you. All the traumas of life have finally left you and you can now get on with your work. It's been a lot of times when you have been tested and tried but now you will reap the rewards of all of your training and letting go. It's not easy to dig deep and look at the past events but it's done now. So you can unwind and smile again. Severe stride and hard work got you there. Facing up to things and listen to others is not always the easiest but you have looked at that now. Life has to go on. So do just that. Now, don't let others rattle you. Whatever they say it's only their opinion. Only believe and we will do the rest. Unfolding time is still here so let it come to you and unfold. Enjoy the little peace and quiet at the moment. It will turn later much busier. Keep taking your herbs and plenty of water for now. Talk less today and ask for a recharge and refreshment. All is indeed well.

Loving calming thoughts from all of us. TttA

OUR FATHER!

By now you know more about your divine father. It's taken a long to understand. Who, what, and where it's all operating from. Don't stop now, you had truth revelation yesterday. As it where you find it hard to accept at times. Leave all that to us again to give you the way to explain it to you. You already have the tools so you can use them when it's needed. The big shiny stones that you are holding in your hands at present will connect you to us and get more energy from the origin of the stone. Let no other human or sub human ever put you off again. It takes steadiness and force to be able to be free to follow through that's why you need spend much time apart and to be able to strengthen your connections to the star system and the universal force and the Godfather. Let us show you the way and lead you in to the green pastures. For our sake as much as yours. So many have started to see your light increase so some try to thwart or disturb you. It's not working any more. Peace and tranquillity are now yours forever.

Blessings and love from all of us. TttA

SURPRISE—SURPRISE!

Let go of thinking that there are no surprises. They still exist is but they are going on at times so you don't even notice what's happened around you. Take a little more interest in small happenings. Yesterday's revelations were quite staggering but necessary to reveal to you. Now you can know what's been going on and make a faster stop or disconnection when necessary. Wolves come in sheep's clothing many times but you sift them out. Perhaps you should do more ghost busting. To be a spirit detective is quite interesting, but always ask for help and the right tools every time. Let go of others so called" know it all". They only want to have more attention because of old neglect and ignore old situations that you feel when feeling uneasy or disturbed. Stop and go away is best. Also keep in mind the stronger you get, the more you will be a thorn in some body's side. Or they will stop trying to put you down. Just stop trying. The person is curious how life works. The sorting is still going on so stay patient. We have your best interest at heart. Take heed.

All our blessings and you did survive once more. TttA

GOOD MORNING!

Yes indeed that is so. The last weeks have been a hard battle, with so much to clear out but we did it together. The pain of it all will now recede. New time will follow. Also your new tools will help you to connect with family and other sources faster, and last night it was a another good connection with your family. They need you as well as you need them. At last everyone knows that and they are opening up to talk and love. You will see miracles unfold that you never thought were possible. More new people will attend your sessions for the benefit of all mankind. It's all got to do with involvement for the benefit of those that so choose. It's still a free will for all that are not controlled by some negative force, and with or without their knowledge. That's the situation you have to be aware of and stay clear of. Still it's a free choice. Get a little more organized before Wednesday. It will help to save time and energy. It will all change for the better now when things have cleared a lot, so we want to congratulate you for holding out and working under trying circumstances.

Blessings and joy from us all. TttA

LET'S JUST BE FOR A LITTLE WHILE!

It's so important that you understand how much energy you will have to regain after a working session. Surely some might say you will have to back to the source. Yes but remember it's different for different souls. The deeper and more time involved it will take a lot of time to regain. Remember how much you used to give away and were very tired and drained after. That was cause and effect again. You know better now, only 50% and at times you perhaps need 40% to 60 %. It's all according to love and care for yourself also, otherwise you will not have enough for others. Stay organized and keep an eye on your environment. Treat the nature well and it will give you a big harvest. At present time you are opening your eyes and ears wide open. You have put things together so you are better prepared. To be able to stay strong in stormy weather you need strong roots and a lot of flexibility that you know very well. How all that works. The technical help you have asked for is on its way. It will be a long working relationship. Future changes are now in our hands.

Love and light from TttA

PEACE AND HARMONY!

How many times do we have to tell you about just that? If you don't take enough notice you will have to rest for a while. Remember what's really is going on. Today is very mixed energy so stay clear as much as possible. It's OK to ask and query many things. Curiosity is also a time waster but don't overdo it just be able to love and laugh again and again and you will see the result. That's not easy when you are trying so hard to do everything right. Don't try so hard, only do the best you can for now. To be too hard on your self is not the way to love yourself. Remember your deep breathing. It will help you in trying times. Let the rest of the day unfold as well as it's going to be. Patience today is sorely tested. Go on with your task and don't let a little interference spoil your day. Rest in the right kind of input will make your day. All is indeed in hand. Trust and don't get too concerned as we are doing all we can to ease up your situation. Get in to a relaxed mood and all will work out fine. Get your work done whenever you can. It does not matter about tradition too much.

Love and light in full measure. TttA

REMEMBER YOUR THOUGHTS!

Let's talk for a little while about your ability to send out thoughts all over the world. That could be learnt of more people. As long as you are sending out love, light and health all of that will increase. And do not ever think that you by yourself can change too much, that has to come from the universal creator and father through you out to other souls. You are one of the bridge workers and activator. Many others are operating around the world except more in your country because of the interest in spirituality and the meaning of life. Lately you have discovered many more clues and puzzles that you have been questioning for a long time. We were waiting for you to come to a certain level before we could explain it to you in full. Others have also started to look at you in a different light. Most times you already knew what they were thinking and you felt the disbelief their minds. We'll let that go now that you have seen through all that so next thing is to get on with life. You have been asking for better input and it's underway already.

Three new souls have found their way to you, plus others who are positive will return. Blessings for the whole day.

Love and laughter from TttA

DIVINE ORDER!

Let that be a lesson for you all today. To be able to give help and assistance is so important, and the skill is already there. Learn how to apply it and pass on your knowledge. It's coming closer but not quite there yet. Let today's work bear fruit. You know your life is changing, so be patient. The angels this morning came and told you so. Trust that that is correct. There is time for everything that's important. Your work colleague is soon to enter a very interesting chapter and he will never look back. Heaven is rejoicing with you both today. We do understand how much you want to go on with your work, and you are. Some do not understand what you are going through. That does not matter at all. You think it's time now, but others involved for future work are not yet ready. Rest assured there is a future for you as well. It's been a long time to sort and sift all but you are doing fine, letting go of so much. The clearing out will give space to have room for new input, so leave all that to us. Blessings be upon you. We are very near just now after the others finally have gone.

Blessed be and thanks. TttA

CONNECTIONS!

Check how and when you connect. It's quite important at this time. So many are hungry for life, and energy that goes with it. They will try anyone or anything for an input. That's not right and it will have an after effect. The person will not grow spiritually or advance on their path. It's important that you do your own work and listening in to us and the living energy that only can come from the universal spring of life. Little do they realise that all they have to do is to connect to the source and then advance enough to let that alter your whole life and then that will be spirit in charge. Above all else of course the youth will come again. That is how you will find out about the fountain of youth. It will take a lot of discipline and hard work, not to settle for less than the real thing. Let the day unfold and relax in between. Don't let all the work that's needed to be done dampen your spirit. Connect today one way or the other with people that need input from the source. We will let you know how to spread the words to them.

Blessings and lots of love and support from TttA

WHEN TWO OF YOU ARE TOGETHER!

Yes I have promised to be the third. Always think of the promises when on Earth and after. Check and believe that I am. So many rely on the worlds of wisdom and other people. Try to go yourself to the source, you might not at first but do try. Practise and more practise will strengthen and get closer to the source. Human conditions are so frail at times and so many are in the mist. That's not good. Keep on sending out love and light to the whole world, and one day it will be clearing all around the globe. Even if you don't see it clear keep on sending out with love from your heart and that's the only way to save the planet. All these confusions at present time disturb so many and they don't know what to do. All you have to do is to let us know. And we will deal with it. Many times you feel helpless and don't know what to do. So just do it. Your next book title will intrigue that is good, and so will the cover, given to you from us. The aim is not for you to know at this point. All in good time.

Blessed be and support always TttA.

MUSIC FROM THE SPHERES!

Heavenly music from us will guide you, under your way to eternity and in the garden of delight. Do not try to see more then what is necessary for your own good and also it's different for people according to where they are and what lesson has to be learnt. So many think what is good for one is good for all? At times it could be so, and do please check and when it's right you know. In the still ness of the morning, you easy can get connected but also we know you that you are more receptive then. So that's another reason why you need discipline. And to have your life in order. The little story about the cat he will carry on with peace from you to his original owner. So one more way that we can use to carry out spreading harmony and healing to more places. The wider the circles of positivity the further it will spread the same old wisdom but another picture for the people, so it can be understood in your land. That is what we mean by being flexible so you always can get through to people. Ask for a picture and we will give it to you.

Blessings and love from us all TttA

TO BE OR NOT TO BE DISCIPLINED!

Yes you must let other things go away, for the mean time and let us be your teachers. When we said to be there for us do so. Well now, you are trying but it all takes time, so you now need to think it all through. So much got side-tracked but the work is still being done. Too many interests and subjects you did your explanations for the events yesterday. Be more vigilant. Clear all with our help, before entering your door. It's so easy taken for granted. You did ask us to clear the people so you can rely on that. Also ask for your aura to be clear, you need more time away with us. As you get more clear and put things together the clearer it gets. Clearing and pruning days are here, so do just that. Sorting out what's needed is fine and knowing where it is and can be found when needed. Your new angel input will serve you well. The higher realms are willing to assist you, so feel reassured that all is in hand. Tonight will prove interesting. Not many will come but the ones that do will have a lot to think about. A little input every week will make a great picture and enlighten others.

Courage my friend the Maori people will soon need you.

Blessings and love TttA

KEEP GOING!

Please understand that you need keep going to be able to reach you goal. Don't let anything put you off or disturb you. It's a big task in front of you, and that's why you have had so much time apart from everyone. Carry on as it's not so easy at times but you are so determined, so it will happen. We will keep an eye on your lost properties and all will be well. It was only interference from some not so likeable force. Today it's another sunny day with bird's butterflies and other of nature's sounds. Do not get in to comparing or concern yourself with little happenings as you don't know the future, it's still pending on other events. Stay calm, collective and cool. Back to the word balance. You will benefit from that in the long term. The scale of justice is about to get activated. Articles that have been taken from you must be returned. Your group will also benefit showing respect and commitment. The word will spread and you will be surprised how many will come and learn. Still remember to check and do what we have told you. Rest and relax for the rest of the day.

Blessings and love from us all. TttA

TODAY IS THE DAY!

Let's not wait any longer. It's action time. So much is not going to be made clear in the spiritual, mental and physical realms. The deeper the issue the longer most people put it off. It's so easy to do and care for others instead of dealing with your own situations. That's human but not to be followed if one wants to proceed higher and deeper. Well now, you might think that's not to be judged or looked down upon. Only to notice and ponder upon. Ask yourself what's for me today to deal with. At might be nothing at times but that was is what divine timing is all about. When you surrender early in the morning. You are leaving it to us so then divine timing activated. It is for us to activate you so don't try to work it out. Rest assured that we have your best interest at heart and that the book of life is keeping a record of all the thoughts and actions and evolvements. Your concern for others is inbuilt in you, so keep it up, but leave the work to us and we let you know if anything needs doing from your end.

A downpour of blessings to all TttA

FOR THE GRACE OF GOD!

The Grace is a very important part of your growth. The full understanding of that word will get you further up on your ladder to enlightenment. Another word is refinement. Most of your living days you are working on letting go. Understanding, insight and refreshment are very important, and to be able to peel off the outer layers is not an easy task, but you are doing just that. The further you go on your upward climbing the better the view and away from all pollution, of spirit mind and body was not meant to be easy, and the steps of learning is to be just that. You all might have different tasks every lifetime, but the journey of the soul is individual. That way you can't compare with anyone or anything. Some have deeper and harder lessons but the soul chose to do the learning and clearing for just that lifetime. So many do not accept that but that's not for you to say, leave that to us. We give the lessons out and give advice for the homework for each individual. Humans are made that way so they can use tools given to them and open their hearts and mind to store and use whenever it's needed or wanted. So keep up your writings and sessions.

Love eternal from TttA

REVELATIONS!

Yes you are finally getting a deeper insight of the universal law, and how easy a miracle can happen. Only belief and surrender to the source and let them deal with it. When you are letting the spirit be in charge most physical conditions will go. It's so hard to fully leave all when you are used to a certain pattern. Habits die hard for most, only determination and divine healing is the best solution to be able to leave all brain activities for a little wile is a struggle for many also. Only by asking for help will come humans are used as tools guided by the divine light. Stay very patient, cool calm and cool for now. We are helping but because of your system we have a different timeslot in mind. It will also remind you about the individuality of all souls. Try to see all as we do. Without any emotional feelings of hurt or damage. It will take a lot of time apart with us, to strengthen your whole system, and also even out your aura field, including your buffer zone.

Support and love always. TttA

GREETINGS!

Once again we have been so close, but no writing for 4 days. Well now we know why, so much clearing out on all different levels. Now you are all clear once again too many areas and tribulations but you got thought it all. It has taken you many years and lifetimes to get where you are today. We rejoice with you today. We will always be there for you, to give you wisdom grace and health. Let today be a day of joy, peace and harmony. To help you to understand and why how and what's has been going on for such a long time. It's so nice that you have accepted that the future for you is not for you to see too far ahead. We will take care of all that for your highest good. People will come to you now for a different reason. That will show you that you are working on the path meant for you this lifetime. A lot of questions that you don't know can now be answered. One part of the time of so many different levels of wisdom. Your father is also beginning to know who you are. Because of you being an indigo child they did not reach you where you were.

Lots of love from TttA

ORDER!

Get yourself in to divine order. It's not as easy as earthy order but more important. Work from that prospective and you will be o.k. and don't try to change or alter anything that we give you. That would be interfering from you, and that you might feel that you know better. That's human but not divine order. Empty out and refill from us that is divine order. Look up and try to visualise the court of divinity. Handling everything stream very professionally and bringing in all in to order. Only by letting that happen will you go ahead and achieve much faster. After, you will understand that we have your interest at heart and teaching you to know when to do what, and who to cooperate with and help guide or enlighten whatever is wanted. You are still a go between and a good one at that. Keep up the work. We also have other areas that we want you to work on in the near future. The learning is still going on and always will be. Back to not having still waters closed up. Inlet and outlet must cooperate so you can be re charged and renewed, always in the making, learning one lesson and then go on to the next. Just like eternity and the figure 8. No beginning, no end, always moving like a stream.

Love and care from us all TttA

LEARNING TIME

Always more to learn otherwise you would stagnate and old age would be the result. That's not for you. Keep on learning, understanding and enlighten and open your spirit heart and mind to be able to connect and learn more every day to add to your wisdom and growth. Don't try to hard little at the time. Knowledge is fine but how to apply. Only it to be wise is quite a different process. That's why you need to spend time apart with us to be able to digest wisdom and know two differences. Ponder and meditate over these two words. We will help you and open up areas that have not been in use for a while. As your seasons are changing you also will change. More inside work and opportunity to go deeper still. That will benefit you in future work and make you more accessible for the right people. That's been asking for certain help in connecting work and understanding were they are. Go on for the rest of the day reading, relaxing and resting. There is plenty of time, to learn and be involved. Healing is given every day.

Blessed be child of light. TttA.

LEARNING EVERMORE!

Let's talk about lessons that you have seen and learned from lately! At times you need to look from a different angle to be able to see what's going on. A fresh outlook is very refreshing as speeding up the truth to help to remember how it all worked before. All in its all good time and rest in between. That does not matter time is manmade to help you to have some kind of order in your life. The energies and weather is still changing do bear with it a little longer. Steady as she goes says the captain of your own ship. Don't let anyone or anything sway you at this point in time. Do your daily work for the source and your own growth. People will arrive at your place for a different reason and some come just for a place to rest a little while. Physical ailment might be present but they are very temporary. Patience is still at the fore front. Tell others to stay close to the source the closer the better for protection care and energy input- equal meaning life force. Back to simple ground rules, let's stay together.

Love and light from TttA

RAYS OF SUNSHINE!

Let's soak up that together. We all know how much you all need all that energy and life giving recharging. Some sunshine every day is most valuable for all. Try not to look to far ahead. It's in the making and you will be pleasantly surprised of the outcome. By the time your other connection you will notice a big change in your way and how you look. Your inside light is growing day by day so that will also help you to come in to your position. The present conditions will also go. You have been through a remaking time but it was necessary for your new work. We know how you feel at times wondering when it all will end, but it was to test your faith in us and the source. Enjoy the sunshine today and your beautiful garden. Yesterday's happening was O K but you were a little tense no need for all that but understandable. Look at the changes already made and it will be more. Live in our company and stay close to the source of all life. Talk to us and let the peace in your heart stay forever.

Blessings and love from us all. TttA

SILVER RAYS AND GOLDEN RAINS!

Look upon to the night sky. We are sending you wings and signs from the source. When you ask questions we send you answer in many ways and forms. The once that comes to your door is sent by us. Many different colours and credo not query why we have sent them, you know by now that we select the comings and goings. It's a purpose with it all and you will hear more soon and also finally see. The need is great and you have gifts to give them different from many others that are also working for the light. You were born that way so thank us for that and much more. It's there to be used for the good of all mankind. And help many in deep distress. Remember to clear after each connection and take time out you have been waiting for this time out to eventuate and at last it's here. Many difficulties at this time for the earth to endure yet. It's part of the clearing and it will get more crises yet. Stay vigilant, steady and flexible. Many will not believe you but it's none of your concern.

You already know what people think anyway. A guideline to make use of.

Loving thoughts and joy. TttA

AUTUMN SUNSHINE!

We welcome your input every morning as you understand we need you to do your part so do just that. No matter what comes we are relying on you as a good scribe. Also remember that when you give out to others that's not your words or deeds only inspired from us to spread love and light to the world. Yesterday's decisions were altered and once again you have proof that all is done in the right order and time. Your wants will be met some other time without any interruptions. Some entities have started to notice your enlightenment so they are trying to get some of it for nothing. That's not acceptable by the universal law so everyone including you must do their own homework. It does not matter when or how, as long as the work is being seriously done. If anyone tries too hard or to push their knowledge it will not work. It's a lot in that as the old saying, "when the students are ready, the teacher will appear" and you know so very well so carry on your part and don't worry too much about the future. It is still being made. Enjoy today and let's do things together.

Love and courage TttA

RELY ON THE SOURCE!

That's the only way you are going to grow and survive. So much confusion is not for anyone. Some said they are from the source partly they are but the other part is from their own ego or mindreading that's OK in one way but not to be followed by others. That is not to be judged, only to take notice of and learn from. Well now so many different and so many so called truths are present on Earth. It might increase a little but there are also very genuine souls that do really have a close contact with us and the source. Still we say don't judge. Everybody has to learn and discern what's going on and were to go for the input of wisdom. Keep on going today as you are and still ponder on what we give you. Yes you know that some will only come to you once. That is fine. They are not ready for what's given and need to come later. Mostly confusion and focusing are the two main stoppages. Time will take care of all that. Writing and painting will start to be very useful and the contact is very good.

Lots of love from us all. TttA

HEALING SOUND VIBRATIONS!

That is one more way to heal. Listen to the harmony of the sound waves. Start to dream and relax, focus on the alpha state. That will bring you to most wonderful healing and restore spirit mind and body. All of your parts healing together spirit, mind, emotion and body. It's a chain reaction that triggers the most beneficial dose of input from the spheres, also it will take you away on a journey to us and experiencing a higher level of understanding. How well everything is organised and how easy it will be to connect when you have started after practising a long time, for some others a shorter time. All considering what's involved and how deep the problem is. It's another way to get faster and more lasting healing. Keep on listening to your music and deal with people as you always and always will, so stay tuned and let other time-consuming issues take a back seat for now. The time spent with us is the best start of your day that you can have. Blessings and laughter will come to you through the day.

Blessed be TttA

KEEP ON GOING!

Yes that the big clue of the day. You would know by now how important that is to follow through. Never ever give up. We also would like to thank you for work done and promises kept. The on-going input and learning is activated so leave all that to us. So much is involved in so many areas needed to be changed. Discipline is also playing a very big part of your training. Remember when weary, rest. It will not do you or anyone else any good to grind on regardless.

Keep the balance and understand. It's all for a good purpose for you and mankind. The training is quite severe but you are doing It. Tonight is another night to renew, reach and restore everyone. Your journey is different but you choose to go there so that was very wise. People's reactions will alter but leave all that to us. You still need to spread your work a little more. So do just that. We are giving you the tools so don't concern yourself about when and how. The training is a human invention so that is such. We don't work like that, but in the meantime use it as a tool.

Amen and blessings TttA

SORTING AND SIFTING!

This is a good time for sorting out and finding out what's what. At times it is so easy to let go and continue collecting and hoarding. Your priorities have altered so everything else is doing so as well. To be able to leave room for new input is beneficial and refreshing. Time is of value and also it will save time later when order has been completed. Stay unruffled and calm when adversities arrive. That's a very good test to stay the same whatever occurs. If nothing is eventuating just wait. Understand it's all for a good cause for all mankind. You will fully see the picture when all is unfolded. We do understand your ways, that's why you are so good at your work. Stay persistent and still vigilant. Easter will come with glad tidings so in the meantime do what the daily input is presenting. Your autumn time is here, so more time still to study the seasons and follow through. Yours and our work will increase in size. At the moment it is in a remodelling mode so go on as you are for now. Be patient with yourself and others. It will become easier as you go along.

Blessings and love from TttA

GLAD TIDINGS!

Let all the joy and glad times come up inside you your heart and flow over. It will be a big release for you, and other than that try the same principles. To apply principles that are wise is very beneficial. You have studied for many years and know that's working. Yesterday's solution was very good and you will have more of them soon. Order in the kingdom on earth and in heaven. We are reminding you about the old saying, "so above so below". Old wisdom needs to be reactivated once again, and again. It's so easy to think about new ideas and new wisdom it's an illusion as nothing is new, only turned over and looked at again. Remember to use the tools that we gave you so long ago. They are tools so treat them as such. It's up to who is holding on to them and what energy is used through them. Trust that we are working through you and always let that is your guide. Let the light and love show you the way. The sun just broke through the clouds so it will be for you also. Keep up your work amen to that.

Blessed be TttA

IN THE SILENCE OF THE DAWN!

Let me give you the most valuable gifts to start the day. Peace and back to nature, to recapture the early bird singing and the awakening of nature. Be silent and absorb the energy from it all. Don't plan or try to work out what time or would it be right. Just be and let me talk with you for a little while. I AM. That is what I am and so are you. I and the father are one. And you have that light inside you also. Ask for more light to fill your whole body, so it can shine and show the way for others that are searching for the eternal purple flame. It's so many ways that can be explained to you and different ways for different levels of understanding. If too complex people get tired and need to retreat. Go on giving out what we ask of you. Your effort is noted and you will get feedback, when we think that you would benefit from it. Today will show a little more of who is who. Don't say too much only observe and you will hear the others thoughts faster. It will be an energy saver and lighten your load. Let the day unfold at your own pace.

Eternal support from TttA

LET GO OF ALL NEGATIVITY!

Yes you know too much of all that and what it can do to your physical. The big surrender each morning will start you off on a positive note. Don't try to work out anything that is if you do. Wait, don't you fully trust the source of all wisdom, goodness and light. So much easier but at present time you are weary about the source of incoming ideas and actions That is fine as long as you ask for advice and check with us. So much subtlety in some cases. That's there to test you and make you learn how others try to intimidate or doing some monkey business. That will be exposed later. That is the universal law. Everyone has to work on their own path and do talk to others but don't take in all they say or being told to do. If in doubt wait. The ones that want to convince others with wrong motives will be dealt with. It's after all a free country. Do respect others opinion but don't swallow if uneasy or doubtful. Let the day bring you ease and joy. Spread the good word around.

Blessings and light from us all. TttA

LOVE AND LIGHT!

Yes my children of earth you all need plenty of just that. And also to bring it in to other people's lives'. Let it happen. Also let the love from your heart overflow and do remember your own heart. All of your wounds that need healing and growth. Remember to ask for help and Stop at once if you feel disturbed or my name it will be given at the right time. The divine plan is operating and is keeping it in order. Do not get chaos in to your life. That will cause distrust and fear and would snowball into bigger and bigger situations. Stop at once if you feel disturbance or uneasiness. As your day is unfolding you will see, hear and experience a lot more of why and who. Take notice of signs and thoughts. We will stay close to make sure you are protected and guided. Rest in the peace and harmony with us. Adversity is about so stay clear when we say so. Be as little children trusting the father's care. The big picture is unfolding and you will know what's coming.

Always love and light TttA

SORTING AND SIFTING AGAIN!

Remember to sort things out before it get to tangle. Don't delay it and when you feel spirit moves you. Get your priorities in order. You have done more lately than before. It feels good does it not. Yesterday's cold and wet weather got you to do a lot more inside work. It was some confusion in the electrical system but you already knew what that was. Wait and don't give it any energy what so ever. Keep on working as you are and tonight we will be with you all for whatever is needed. We do like you talking more to us now, and you are working to hear us. The cats see more than you at the moment. Study their ways and enjoy their company. How natural it is for them and they love you for what you are. Your closeness to all animals is noted. You seem to understand better than many. Think calm and calm will come and stay close. Blessed be meek and lowly. As fast as lightning all can change, so stay flexible and alert. We are with you and soon you see. You will like that.

Blessings from TttA

RECONNECTED AGAIN!

Yes, remember to connect and every time you do you get closer to the source. It's OK to rest and take time out but before you do, ask for protection and input. Input and wisdom comes closer to you when you are rested and relaxed. The same goes for priorities. You need to stand back and at times rise above so you can find out exactly what is going on with the prospective of the whole situation. Let go of ideas that are no longer useful to you. At the time when you got them they were a stepping stone for you. Look at them as tools. Your new exercise program will benefit you a lot, and to keep subtle and alert will also aid you in your progress. New tools will also come to you, as you are getting a closer link. As the veil has now lifted you will also hear and later see us clearer. Still we say check, as distractions are around and will try to side track you. We will ring warning bells when.

Always yours TttA

UNFOLDING TIME!

Let it all unfold steadily and in order. Let us do the input, and then let you know what is for the day. The big picture is unfolding as well. Don't try to work it out for yourself and you will still get to your goal. But the cost will be very great and also time is involved. As time is of essence at present, don't delay your work by side tracking or other minor distortions. We in the higher spheres are very busy and also very organised, so all is really in hand. If and when we say wait, do wait and don't make any major changes. Then when all is in order for all concerned the move will occur. You are not puppets. Free will still exist. The choice is to know how to make the right choices by tuning in and listen to your guides and teachers. That is when practise comes in. Don't expect results at once. In certain cases it could happen instantly but mostly it will take its course. Like going back to school. Spirit school works with the same principles as the earth school. Do your homework and all will be well.

Blessings and love. TttA

REJOICE IN YOUR WORK!

Remember to stay calm and positive under adverse circumstances. Yesterday's work was long overdue. The old magician was in need of a reconnecting and real time. Don't work than we ask you leave things to us. We know all his ins and outs. Many similar studies will be made to help you understand and support your knowledge from the past. Again we say to you whatever that comes or connects with you are having a need for answers. Ask us for the replay to give them satisfaction. So many have been way led from many well-meaning sources so fresh start in that case. Many swallow what authority figures present. Stop and ask what's going on. Many times it's a power struggle and ego comes in to it. That's very human but should be looked and validated again. We know they are well meaning but not checked enough. Still we say ask for the need from others to know so they have to come to you. Or others are working for the light. No one should be coerced in to believe.

Blessed be from. TttA

SOAK UP THE LIFE-GIVING FROM THE SUN!

Yes my children of light you need to keep in mind to recharge every day so you can benefit from it and give out more to others. Let it all pass on and remember to keep a part for you. The love and nurturing of the self as many might have said. The think they know but often they are brain washed from one source or the other. Some believe they are just so right but that's' quite naive. Dig deeper to see what the cause is for people's actions and thoughts. Wait if we say so, it's often emotional or mistreatment.in this life or before. The soul memories are very strong for some. Gruesome event left scars. Rather too much of alien influences good or bad so check with us for facts. Still ask us for do the clearance. It's better for you and no after effects. Last night's events were so obvious to you but you handled that well.

Blessings and wisdom from TttA

A NEW DAY!

Yes my lighthouse worker. Make sure you have everything ready for shining the light to others. You know that to be able to let the universal light go through you from us. Prepare the way and let us deal with the supplies. Anything honestly meant from the heart will give you whatever you need if you don't ask for it. My storehouse is full don't ever let pride or inhibitions block what you're asking for. We have many ways to offer you assistance, and we know who will practically give it from us to you. Yesterday you could see many examples of just that. Remember it's only given if and when it will benefit your growth and also encourage you to go ahead. All work for the source is never forgotten or unaccounted for every little thing honestly meant from the heart are valuable. You might not always see, the result but we do. Not that is have to be perfect but the best possible way that you can from your level of understanding. You have. Also when you have done your best and not finished, we will. Don't over stretch yourself.

Warmest blessings and love from TttA

ALL IN MY NAME

That's what we say. I am that I am and always will be.Remember long ago when we were talking and walking about life and the universe. That wisdom can always be used again and again. There is not anything new at any point only reused and recycled and reborn. So many are looking for new ideas thoughts and beliefs. Curiosity and not having enough faith is the culprit. Also remember to talk with people I send to your door. The only thing might be a little word or a smile. That person is or wanted just that. Time is speeding up and you would do well to listen in for when or what to do. Easter time is coming up and a new energy will emerge. Be still and observe. So many changes are occurring and you are altering as well. Rest when finished your work and just be. Look around you and see the season's change. Listen to the sound of nature and rejoice that all is good order. We are very near at this point.

Eternally yours! TttA

ENJOY THE MOMENT!

Yes you will benefit from just that and also take care of today. On a grey day you will remember the sunny days and fresh air. Soon you will understand more and situations will fall in to place and you will reach more people. Let the little interferences go, they are only there to test and check out what your actions are when they come. Do your very best to see what we are trying to communicate to you. Your perceiving percentage and your accuracy is improving. So keep going and you are going to do work for us with unlimited powers, and let us give you more tools to use for a fast recovery. More students will come and we say ask us to check every body. People that have come to you lately really do listen and respect you. Let that be a start to your new life, advertising a risen Christ at Easter. All the signs are there and at times you don't look close enough so you have not used the deeper and higher communication lines. Still stay vigilant and we are still guarding you and your life. Always surrender all you have to do is ask, specifically first is best.

Love and care from TttA.

REJOICE!

Once more I say rejoice for all the health clearing and cleaning that has been done. You are now able to see faster what's going on, you have been searching for a long time now and in many different areas. To be able to find out what's going on. You have found out quite a lot so more will come. In your case you want to keep on preparing what we want you to do for next week. More souls are walking in the mist are finding their way to your sanctuary. That is good and coming at the right time Still send out love light and laughter to all. Do not pick out them they all want to feel the heavenly care through you. Most need s signs or experiences to believe to understand what has been so confusing in their lives. Nothing is for nothing in life. You will understand more as you go along and open your heart and soul to the truth. All the once that treated you negatively are being dealt with. It was not of their making only to thwart you in your work. All did do you a favour to work even harder.

Easter tide is flowing in. TttA

EARLY START ONCE AGAIN!

Remember to do most work early when you have just heard back from us. Refreshed and renewed. That's what is going on through the night. It was a very good session last night. All that was meant to be and asked to be cleared for good. That will mean so much support, and more cooperation. Still be vigilant and we know you are. Hatching and waiting for new happenings and what is on the horizon. Old friends will now return in a different form. Welcome them back, the ones that do not appear again will be replaced by my new students of light. Your connection overseas will also understand more and you will hear feedback from long lost souls. The music of the spheres that your love and light has sent out so many times will also increase. Keep on your work. We are so pleased with your progress and the new found joy that you are feeling. It has touched your heart so you can get rid of more scar tissues. Blessed be and keep on climbing.

Love and light from. TttA

AGAIN AND AGAIN!

Remember that repetition is the well of all knowledge and the source of the well. Think of that many times that you nearly given up and something or someone and all is well again, that is what we call the spirit law. You are learning that and now it's up to you how much longer. A little bit at a time will do it and stay vigilant and persistent you will know when the time is right. Enjoy interaction today and you have started to feel it's an end to it all. Go careful and don't hurry anywhere. Easy does it, Look around you and see how, your pets are behaving they are one of the most natural teachers there are. Start to organize your new book and ask for assistance how to best deal with it all the details. Today's lesson will be very beneficial and useful. My healing touch will always be with you. And with the ones that come to you. They will feel a need to come back for more and understand how important that is to connect with us. Relax and feel at ease you have just now been in a battle. And come through in one peace. Onwards and upwards.

Cheer and love. TttA

FREEDOM!

To be able to work and act in freedom is a valuable gift. Don't ever forget that you know all of that from the past. So use it for the good of all mankind. Think of the work as a step up. Practise and practise will get you there. All information and all tools will be given and will be used. Remember different tools for different jobs. And the right dosages. So many situations and so much cleaning needs to be done. So all that's trained for that special kind of work will soon get more tools. And a clear line to us for clears access. To knowledge and information's and help of all different kinds. Don't be too sure that you have checked enough. Or don't need protection. The energies and the latest news are also disturbing to many. Only still do what we say, and take our advice. Healing and realignment is in process. Stay with it, and all will be well. Students will come when requested or need a little more input. To be able to understand the pattern. Ask for more signs.

Always yours forever. TttA

JOY FOR EASTER

Cheer up so much to be grateful for and so many miracles already. The big clean and clear up, is in full swing. Bear with it and be grateful, and count your blessings. Your heavenly father is the father of all. The Christ in me salutes the Christ in you. My father and I are one. We all have been given the knowledge and the god spark to be able to live and work. Without the father you could not get activated or activate others. Let it all pass over to the hungry ones that are waiting with open arms and hearts. Let go of woes and worries, give them to us that care and love you. Go easy on yourself and love and support each other. So much of the healthy enzymes will be released when you smile and forgive. Let go and let live. Trust and surrender to all living and giving forces of the universe and all will be well. Today more peace will enter your life and make the more concerned connected.

Easter joy and new flow of life from. TttA

REST AND RECHARGE!

Remember to have a break and let the restoration of soul mind and body take place in a natural way. Don't be fooled or tempted to change that. You know very well how easy it would be to alter the course. Don't delay your actions or put off the whole issue. The best you can do is to follow our advice. The sun is always there even if you don't see it. The same about us, we are also always there, even if you don't always feel us. Remember that the pattern is spiritual and universal. So that's the law of heaven. Always the same eternally. Let that sink in to your sub conscious and remind you about us and the teachings. This morning you got another reminder of negative control. Some people are getting these also and are so used to it that they don't even check and think what's going on and not harming natural life. Only controlled life. That's becoming the normal life to them. So what will be the solution? Stop and get off the merry go round. Too much energy is going away for nothing. Ponder on that.

Eternal blessings TttA

HUMANITY AND COMPASSION!

Yes my children of light should do just that. My light and my love will sustain you and keep your spirit alive to be able to pass on to others from us. Remember that you have tools and channels for your everlasting universal love and light source. Also keep in mind what we so often have told you. Wait if we say so, trust and faith are also the main ingredients of growth and deeper understanding while you are living. In order to extend your spiritual growth and to spend a great time in meditation and prayers it is necessary for a good connection between the dimensions, the communication between teachers, healers and prophets and all students will become closer, and you honestly just have to ask and we will be there. Your autumn weather has arrived so prepare for the next season and all preparations will be used and you will have reason to be grateful that you have filled your lamps with oil. Stay alert and trust that all is well. Keep on with your studying. It will bring result.

Love and Easter blessings TttA

EASTER MORNING!

Today I have risen once again. You know, but also remind others about the empty tomb. So very few did know and did not believe what was going to happen. I did my very best for all and they did not understand me and also the priests were against me as they are against you many times. To still have the courage to follow through takes focus and work. In your case you are doing more than we aspect of you, but that's you. Today is a recharging day and you are outside in the sun, listening to your birds, and a few bees are still around. The autumn weather is still quite good but the cold is coming in at night. Keep warm and practical. We know your physical system very well.so don't push it. Keep asking for help and it will be given. Your new treatment is good for you, activation was needed. Keep an eye on your intakes. Moderation in all things. We are standing by now and we have for a long while. There is interference about, but we shield you as best as we can. No big detox in your case, only top up of energy and calming thoughts to all. All is in good working order.

Blessings and light. TttA

TODAY AND YESTERDAY!

Yes my friend they all are in a line that is why things have to go together. Today's action will bear fruit. You don't know yet, but it will be a turnaround for him. To fully accept is hard for many, but time does not matter. Where there is progress to be made. Otherwise it's all important. Don't waste too much time trying to solve problems. That's out of your reach. Hand them back to us to deal with. You are learning just that, so keep it up. Healing of spirit mind and body are activated stronger so you can do more work for the light. We know that you trust now, so now you are completely safe and accepted wise for yourself and others. Today's warmth and love from us will also help to restore your faith and trust a little more. Do not concern yourself for the way things are going and from were help is emerging. Only check with us for us to be there for you and to keep you calm and settled. Be a living proof of me and your team and reflect your lord and helper.

Amen to all that. TttA

DIVINE TIMING!

Let's think about time as it is man made on Earth. That's only because you need to have an order to guide you. We only count in divine time. So when it's all in the right moment it will happen. So many are trying so hard to make time or when they can know about when and how. Instead of asking the divine source, always go to the source for all your queries and rely on your input that will be given. Nothing should be done in a hurry, only at times there is an emergency. Good work and advancement takes time. You know best the time slot that is working for you. Not always someone else's timing. The story about clocks that are going too fast, or too slow and are never showing the right time. The only one time is showing the right time once a day is the one that stopped? Well now that is so. What about father time. The old Merlin was him, and it's good to know the meaning of time. Remember the parables are there to help and guide you.

Eternal love and light from TttA

BALANCE!

Yes my earthly children of light remember to do just that. Too much of anything is not good. This morning you experienced that once more. When you see its coming change the subject. So many are trying to get your energies, not really yours it's ours. They are unplugged when they do just that. All of you would do well to remember to stay plugged in. To disconnect from the source could cause you to get depleted. Watch out for the warning signs the natural balance is to be looked at. It's very important part of everyone once growth. It's the only thing that makes you have discipline. The law of the universe and the spirit is always the same and always will be. You can rely on the order, what you saw will come up. One way or the other. The balance is always the answer for most queries. Think and wait until you understand what the principles are. Rest and recharge for the rest of the day.

Amen to that. TttA

HOLY WAR HOLY DEFENCE!

Let's be together once again. By now we know that you are fully aware of what's going on, and you would do well to encourage others to learn and advance. Today and yesterday we have been close to you. And helped and checked you over. You are now qualified to do our kind of cooperation work and time is still short. So we ask you to be very hopeful vigilant and do as requested. Some years yet but as you know a lot of work is ahead. Your group is enlarging and your one to one communication also. That is what we told you and now is the time. All the tools and energy is provided and you are very secure and a good student. It's been a long time coming so much has been cleared and cleaned. You are no longer the same person or have the same ideas and habits as before. Many years of learning, understanding and accepting. No one get ahead on their on their own and no one can advance further if you don't do your homework. Spirit leaching is forbidden and will have repercussions if they try.

Blessings and love from TttA.

KEEP PLUGGED IN TO THE SOURCE!

Everyone needs to remember to plug in to the source, not to somebody else. That's what is called spirit leaching. That is to be lazy and idle not to do their own homework, only what's given to you part of work that's needed for human connection. We do rely on you all that are working for the eternal purple flame. Let the flames of health wealth and happiness burn ever increasing. Every time you follow through you are putting another log on the fire. Keep the home fires burning and alive. Take care not to overdo things. Remember to recharge yourself and reactivate your tools. All you have to do is to ask us and we will give all the necessary advice and input. Trust and faith will supply all your daily needs. Remember also to keep in close contact and always be plugged in. Do not tempt faith or get slack on your work. Priorities must be looked at every day. And don't concern yourself about tomorrow. That is not for you. Every day is a change to live so fully as possible.

Lots of energy and love from TttA

TWO DAYS TOGETHER!

Once again two days has gone, but at least we know why. Busy days again! Well we did tell you to fill your lamps and tidy up loose ends. You have been so busy, only a little way to go. As a lightning from above, you have seen heard and evolved fast. Like we have said many times before when the spirit moves, it really moves! Yesterday it was another connection, all proven to be very beneficial. You watched and waited and then the miracle. It's all true and you will see more of that later. We know how much you want to see so we are having a meeting to see when and how. Stay patient and vigilant. Saturday will bring some news of unexpected nature. Follow through what we give you, and all will be well. Trust that the picture is all in hand. If it looks confusing stay with it and it will be revealed in time. Work on your book and everything will come out in the light, as well as other situations that needed to be sorted.

Today will also prove to be rewarding. Blessings and hope from all of us. Thanking you for the scribe work.

Blessed be from TttA

CALM AND PEACE!

Let it be calm and peaceful everywhere. So much depends on just that. When storms and raging appear always keep smiling and give out love. We trust you and fully rely on you to fulfil your task on earthly time. You are fully supported at all times. And we are giving you all your tools, and all you require. Also healing, wisdom and love. Your little insecurities and old conditions still have a little hold on you, but it is getting less apparent. Do some more paintings and keep our daily contact close. Last night's input will increase and you will be a big blessing for many searching souls. Fully trust that your healing in all areas will be completed. It's a long time but we all have to test your patience and balance. So far, so good. It's not always going to be so hard, easier times later on. Keep on writing, healing and get invigorated. Feel safe and protected and loved in all four areas.

Lots of love support and wisdom from TttA

ENJOY THE LIGHT AND LOVE!

Yes my child you are doing a lot more light work and you can now become what you was meant to in the first place. It's been a long time coming but now when it's here, you are who you are, and we have always known what you were going into the future to the light. Let us keep up filling your vessels and you will pass on what's needed. We are rejoicing with you about the work that was done this morning, in the name of the light. They in their turn will pass on to others and spread the light further. That's a whole lot of drain work, one fits in with the others a long chain of work for souls on earth. One day you will have another close look, and see the changes and understand what all the training was all about. Still you will see ahead and do tell if and when you get the picture to pass on. It's up to them not your task, how it's taken. Don't alter anything we know that you are following through to the best of your abilities. Let the day unfold as it may.

Love and light always. TttA

GOOD AFTERNOON!

What a great day! Today you have experienced a lot more input from spirit. We rang your bells 5 times to let you know we are rejoicing with you for souls getting closer to the light. We gave you all the tools and told you when an who need to experience the healing powers of your crystals. The old man needed to feel the force before his final time this lifetime on earth. You listened and surrendered this morning. Also when you surrender in the early hours in the morning, stay close also with the little bear he is finding it hard at times but he will understand more later on after developing further. Thank you for doing the task that we needed you for. We said to be flexible and that's what's going on when you deal with other people. The beginning of closer family connection is helpful. Carry on as we give you work. Don't concern yourself about the timing; ask us to sort that out. Likewise with your other queries. It's all in hand so rest and recharge tonight before next lot.

Eternal love and light from TttA

ALL IN GOOD TIME!

Lately you have cause to think about that. You have seen all sorts of events taken place and wondered why. Now you know better. Things are unfolding in the front of your eyes very fast, and you might remember to take time out and be alone with us, your teachers and healers. This morning went as well as yesterday, very much a feeling of movement and falling in to place. Don't leave things that spirit prompts for too long, as priorities are to be taken into consideration and small tasks could be done later. Also take time out between tasks to take a deep breath and meditate.

It will restore you very fast, and we will let you know how often and when right moment is here. Listen in and follow through and all will be well. The group is also evolving in thoughts in wondrous ways. The lovely thoughts and actions this morning will benefit the whole group. A little change here and there will lift the whole energy field and make everything more enjoyable.

Many blessings and thoughts for the day from TttA

ALTERATIONS AND RENEWING!

Well now the storm has got you going, and you got inspired. That's a very good thing, because things were about to get into a stagnated mood. All that swapping and giving released a lot of good energy. You will notice more and more how life is changing for you and quite a lot of others. To learn how to evolve is very beneficial, and freed many ideas that you will use for the future workload. Don't query your input if you don't know the whole picture. Surrender to us in the morning, and night, we see that your faith and trust have increased greatly. The work that you need is given now and will give you increasing circles of big knowledge. Others will come and sit, and others will get what is required. We don't need to tell you that anymore. When you ask us to be present, you will get our support and a faster solution for all involved. We also have given you all the tools needed and all other aspect that's suitable. We'll now so much happened in a very short time so go easy for the rest of the day to get ready for tonight.

Always love and light from TttA

A CLEAR VIEW!

Clear away everything that's blocking your view. Otherwise it will stop you from seeing the full picture. That picture is so important for your understanding for what we are telling you. If and when you are tested, it will show you more blockages on the horizon. Keep an eye on what's on your path. Do not ever think or believe that you are not being tested. The more often you get tested it's a sign that you look closer at what's going on. We still will stand by you but you must learn to make a good judgement of character, where or to what degree they are working or belong. Controlled or not controlled, be ever so vigilant as before but more widely alert. We are giving you very strong support at these changing times. At all transmission times you are more vulnerable. So take care of all four areas. And a little more time out. Yesterday's enlightenment was important for further work. Still work on discipline and focus. We were with you last night to do a big clean up and help you next day.

Courage and love from us all from TttA

STAY CLOSE TO THE SOURCE!

Beware of even a slight pull away from the generator-the source. We do understand how things are at present time, but it's only temporary. You got another glimpse how people operate when not genuine. When some to appear and it's not it will come out sooner or later. Only the real and honest souls will stay with you, also meaning with me or us. A few days now you have been given a picture to which was explained to you. How to find the genuine and how long time before the others will be exposed. You are getting better at spotting who is who. This is good but still we say, see the good in everybody, like we do. Quite often that are souls that have been tarnished with the wrong brush, or been taken control of by some other force without knowing it, and then wonder why their actions have changed. Beware of operating on your own, and not being plugged in to the source. Danger awaits you if you don't, or it could be considered an ego trip. First class! Don't belittle yourself, only forgive yourself. Still love yourself and others will love you. From the source. Ponder on all that today. Enjoy your life.

Love and light always. TttA

EQUALIZE!

The situation needs to be balanced and equalized. Not too much or not enough is always best. Tread carefully on your path. So many people and connections are involved, so keep on asking us for help and support. You as well as many others are only tools, and together with what we give you will learn about other useful tools. The work will be done to everybody's satisfaction. The different levels of development are obvious for us. Study and learn and you will be the same. Observe the lessons that we are giving you, and ask if you don't understand. We are surrounding you so close for protection and other input. Present condition for some, will be resolved. Today's event will also have a good result. The sun and the fresh air will also recharge you. The new growth in your garden is also a sign. That the growth is going on in you to. The pets are also feeling the changes. You are more disciplined now and focused so keep it coming. Also try to typing for your other book is most valued. Keep the order.

Lots of love and light from. TttA

ALL IN GOOD TIME!

The divine diming is so important. You on Earth think that all things that you want to do are done when you want them, but later on you will see that was not so. Divine timing is events and actions that happen for the good of your life, and spirit growth. Today's very many meetings were inspired by us, and activated from the higher realms. Carry on with today's tasks and connect with us every time you work. Never feel that you don't do all that you are given you are and more you do. We are giving you the wisdom and strength to do it all in our name. Blessed are the meek and lowly. The last few weeks are so much more involved and your life. That's why you have taken so much with quite time for so many years. To be able to be ready. Back to the divine timing and order. Day by day you are learning how important your part is. The same goes for your books. We are giving you the wisdom and energy. We also are protecting you fully. Amen to that. Keep up the water intake and rest in between.

Sunny greetings from us all. TttA

PONDER ON LIFE!

Where does it go and where do I go. The next step seems far away, if and when that arises, stop and surrender to the source. If you are too close to a situation stand back and rise up like an eagle to get a bird's eye view of the situation. Most souls get tangled up in this crazy dimension of yours. That's all changing in time, so much clearing and cleaning up. A lot of negativity and old stuff is hanging around. All of that is now surfacing, and have done so for a long time.

Try to see life as going back to school and learn how life is operating in your case. We all are getting lessons, so learn. That we have reminded you so many times. We will keep on doing so when we think you could do with it. Repetition is always the core of learning. Try also to understand divine timing. That's the only thing that is the reliable thing that you all can count on? You are told about members coming to your group and now you see its many cobwebs of your world. Call us and the angels to assist you and you know we will.

Blessed be from TttA

PEACE IS WITH YOU ALL!

Let our loving peace enter your soul and stay there. In this time you all need of just that. Stay calm and let the world pass by. Growth is not easy done for some but discipline and focus will get you there. Like we have said many times before go back to school and do your homework. Tonight's sessions will be very interesting and rewarding. So many on Earth are lost and attacked or walking in a maze. Too much influence from other sources. When someone is vulnerable they will become an easy target. Help each other out and you all will something very good Stop asking who you should help. We all have that in hand. So watch who is coming to you or who is contacting you. We have prompted them to ask you and you will give them our answer. All of you have a part to play in the big picture. Do only yours others should do the same. We will watch over your work.

Love in full measure. From TttA

ALL IN ORDER AND TIME.

On earth you have your own ideas when or what things should be done. That might be so but you would be wise to listen to our good adviser. There are many ways to leads to Rome as the saying goes but don't get side-tracked it will only delay you to go the extra miles for no good reason. Straight and narrow is the best way, lonely at times, but that is so meant and standing back and get on with the job. The life as it has been is no longer in use to help and control you. A better and brighter time after all that clearing out more and more. You are surrendering to us twice a day. We are your healer's teachers and strength. The Earth movement is still on going. Stay flexible. The new energy input from us was very timely, more energy was needed from more student of light, our students. Thank you for open your heart and home to us. We know how much you want to work for the universal light and support and heal all living things in the name of Christ.

Amen to all that. TttA

REJOICE FOR ALL WORK WELL DONE!

Thank you once more for keep the writing going. This morning is another mile stone passed. It's good to achieve tasks and go on to new once. The never ending story about life and how to handle it for the best. You have now worked for many long years and got a lot of progress in that time. Don't ever look back and wonder about your choices. They were made from your understanding at that time. Now you can get on to tell others about your experiences that gave you a lot of knowledge and you got closer to the source and us. So all in all it was for the best. No one should control others, they all have to learn and study for growth and understanding. If you only knew how much easier life will be when you surrender? And ask us for help and when someone was trying to tell you what to do without being asked they only meant well but stopping you to finding out and learn. That is called cosmic interference. Beware and learn. Keep your work up with the typing.

Wisdom and light from us all. TttA

REFRESH AND RESTART!

Remember to start a little earlier from now and on. You are refreshed after coming back from your visit with us. Use that time for your new book and let it all unfold naturally. Don't try to go against the wind it will only result in loss of energy and time. Stay flexible at all cost. Yesterday it was another proof that you can cope with many situations with our help. Now when you have past one more test, we will give you knew once. Back to learning and open up to our wisdom and trust, faith and charity will speedily come your way. Let todays blessings come with renewed strength. We are always beside you and protecting you. We know the plans for you but we will only tell you what you need for now. More situations with more work is coming your way so rest and relax in between. And all will be well. Our storehouse is overflowing with all things so ask and it will come. Lighten up a little we understand why you are feeling as you are that was a part of the transition. Today, a big workload will empower you. Keep up the water intake.

Blessings in many folds. TttA

START AGAIN!

Remember to have a rest and then restart next thing. It's in the eternal pattern. Look back when regrouping and see clearer what's going on. Never be too close to a situation when looking at it. Stand back and empty out, the writing is fine and also the persistence of work is also right. Now and then you did not get time for it all. But we understand. We say ask a little more specific. We all have a lot to do now. Some situations have already been resolved, and others are getting closure. Don't try to push anything or anyone.

No good work will come as a result from frazzled energy. Honour yourself enough to see what's needed and you are not a robot. Nature is bound to take its course whatever you do. Enjoy the little surprises and don't expect to know what you want if you don't tell them. Today's sunshine comes with a warm interruption for you to enjoy. Visualise more sun coming in to you mind and heart. Thank you for doing your part in the light work.

Amen to that. TttA

A FRESH START!

The conditions today are a sign of all the changes in the atmosphere. The whole solar system is in a time of change. Stay with it for now and still be calm happy and loving to all. Don't look to far ahead at present. Not enough areas are settled or sorted. Leave all of that to us and only do as requested. You still have a free will and still learning from the rich source of knowledge. Today's meeting will benefit for all concerned. One more soul that's coming in to the light. That was what we meant when we told you about the pebbles that were strewn upon the waters. The same goes for all similar conditions. Beware who is casting what. Always look at the leaders and forerunners. When you stand back you can see the thread running through it all. Always stand back or better still rise above it all. It's a common saying but not many remember that, when they are too busy or side tracked. Back to balance as always.

Love and light from TttA

A DAY AT A TIME!

Let the day unfold as much it was meant to. Today's event is a sign from the source. The source is alive and very much alive. Keep faith and trust alive and be vigilant always. Condition is really proving to be trying and testing. To be able to see and to hear what's going on is a good sign of growth. Keep going as you are one day at a time. There will be a time when you wonder and ask when STOP. It's not up to you, so surrender and leave it to us. So do just that. Time is only a human condition so do not try to change that to eternal time or universal law. Beware of getting mixed up. It would not get you to understand. What it is all about. Let us deal with your sprit mind and body, also emotions. They all should be working in harmony and grow together. You can never treat anyone in only one area it always reflects on the other parts. That is what we mean when we talk about universal law. Let us be with you and give you support and love for the rest of the day.

Peace be with you from TttA

PEACE IS WITH YOU ALL!

Let our loving peace enter your soul and stay there. In this time you all need of just that. Stay calm and let the world pass by. Growth is not easy done for some but discipline and focus will get you there. Like we have said many times before go back to school and do your homework. Tonight's sessions will be very interesting and rewarding. So many on Earth are lost and attacked or walking in a maze. Too much influence from other sources. When someone is vulnerable they will become an easy target. Help each other out and you all will see something very good. Stop asking who you should help. We all have that in hand. So watch who is coming to you or who is contacting you. We have prompted them to ask you and you will give them our answer. All of you have a part to play in the big picture. Do only yours others should do the same. We will watch over your work.

Love in full measure. From TttA

REJOICE AND TRUST AGAIN!

Let us do just that today. So much has been going on and so much more is to come. You have been asking for years when you will see spirit again. And lo and behold to day you did. It was very good to see at last. It will help you in your work for the light. It was a lost soul that you will see again so many similar cases will be dealt with later. Carry on with today's tasks one at a time and all are well and stay well. Keep up your work with the groups. We are giving you the ones that need to come to you, and other workers will deal with theirs. Let the sun warm and lighten you up. These days you will need to stay very close and visit us at night. You are progressing and we rejoice with you to climb up to the peak. Remember to recharge ad trust again fully. Let us give you more peace and tools so you can check. Let today event help and encourage you and your connections.

Love and wisdom through TttA

CHANGING TIMES!

Yes my children see the pattern and look how many times events are changing at present. That is because so many people are trying to look at their life and trying to see what's going on. So much confusion and so much grief. At times you have felt that all was gone and next minute something else surfaced. It might be so and it can only unfold in one level at the time. We are the only ones that know the truth. We are also the only ones that you can get real help from. Support each other in your human conditions. The whole earth is so disturbed now. Time is speeding up, and so many different styles of beliefs are rising up from everywhere. Still listen and sort and sift out who is who. Stand back and let us deal with the complications caused by jealousy and envy. The same goes for the sun and the stars. Look up and reconnect with the source. That is what you are doing anyway. Only a little reminder. So long as you know.

Tenderness and grace from TttA

TRIALS AND TRIBULATIONS!

Let todays experiences teach you to stay calm and detached. So many different energies in so little space. That is not an easy way in the beginning of the week, but you learned a valuable lesson. Always one thing comes out of the event. Back to the source after and regain your strength you had when visiting us at night. The world as you see it is so different from others. Get in order and when tired leave it alone and back again with us. Your mind is still at times playing games on you. Ask for that to be rectified. Use colour and music and remember to drink enough water. Today is another catch up day, like yesterday. It all has the work in balance. Having your system is not easy, but you are doing what you can to keep all things moving. We are still with you especially at night. Stay tuned in and let the day unfold.as apart of your healing. To change a few things was a good idea. Keep on doing your part of your journey.

Blessings and courage from TttA

ORDER!

Let order and discipline stay with you forever. So much will get lost and ignored because of timing and disorganisation. Don't let it happen to you. The same goes for lessons learned. Try to see the red thread in it all. We have said so many times before but once again strengthen our bonds. The stronghold is very beneficial when the storm rages it will not break. The same goes for the two growths a strong root system will hold, and will hold the tree when anything disturbs the calm and balance. At present time you need to wait, it would be wise of you to follow that line. If and when you don't know the full picture and leave it alone. Some souls could be disturbed if you move too soon. So pray for a sign to know when. Support and nurturing at any level will help you and encourage many. Keep on working with others and for others. When you feel that in certain direction. Don't ask why that's not for you to know at this time. Stand by your convictions and live as you have been advised.

Blessings and joy from TttA

TODAY FOLLOW THROUGH!

Yes do just that, but after take a break. Time out is there for a purpose. Recharging and renewing are the keys for the day. All is well, but when overstretched things could easily get out of order. Remember to relax and smile. Feel good about yourself and others. Do not concern yourself about conditions that are not yours. Learn to pass on to us all of that that cannot be solved by you. Again we say do your part only and learn from it. Time is short but it does not mean not to taking care of yourself and you will do much better input when rested. Do not think that you are not valued enough or don't count. All of you light workers are very much wanted and they all need to be remembering that. Do not make more decisions at present! Too much is going on. Wait a little while and don't think too much. You are very much cared for and loved. That was shown to you last night and you will have proof soon.

Lots of love and laughter from TttA

ONE MORE EXAM PASSED!

Today is an exam of one more section of progress. Do not think that you have not advanced fast enough you have. You have exceeded your quota but far the biggest for you yet. So much has gone away and so new input is needed from searching souls. That was what we meant by explaining to you about going back to school. The school of life. It's a long travel to fulfil your destiny. Many get very tired, frustrated or disbelieving. Understandable but it was not a safety measure involved. Not being plugged in and receiving fresh input is to take a risk. No one can do all that learning without higher wisdom and good teachers. That would only make it an ego trip first class. Listen and learn and you will always know but soon at a deeper level of understanding. Yesterday's event was meant to disturb you and take energy but you manage that very well. Upwards and onwards. Every time that happens you get stronger, so someone would like to trip you up will be tripped up themselves and also they are doing you a favour.

Blessings and health from TttA

LET TODAY BE A DAY OF ENLIGHTENMENT!

The more light that's coming through the clearer the picture about you works will come to you. So many pieces of the puzzles are coming together. When you were only given a few pieces was very hard even to imagine. For every piece from now and on the colours and the different figures will be so much easier to understand. No one can be expected to work without a good chart. The same it is for the captain that is steering his ship away from rocks and dangerous waters. You do know about the stars and how to navigate. The same goes for anyone's journey through life to fulfil your path this life time. No one said it would be easy. Nothing is more worth that a good lesson about methods and discipline throughout the learning. Nothing that's valuable is learnt easily, so with your life. Looking back you did have many practical and mental quests. Many times you were to close so you did not see what was going on. Now you have studied and know how to stand back, to get a better view.

Loving thoughts from TttA.

LET GO OF YESTERDAY!

My child of light you did have a good reminder about inner protection. A time of learning and a time for rest. All in balance once again. Your life looks like others, but it's a big difference. Always do what's right for you. Others might not think so but it's not of any value. Your time clock is so finely tuned in so it takes not much to rattle it, but you are getting better at handling it all. So many lifetimes and so many situations. It's all has been for you to learn from. Don't be discouraged or put off when the entire event does not always come out to your liking. You can't see the picture but looking back you can see glints of it all. You have been asking for something to smile about. Yes we do know, it will come when the divine time is activated. That is why we give you the answer to wait. We will support you and give you hope. When or how it's for us to decide. Keep on surrendering morning and night. Healing and joy is coming your way.

Peace and strength is yours TttA

GOOD WORK IS LASTING!

Well done my child of light. You did have a battle for the last few days. That was necessary for you were understanding and growth you did wonder for a few months but not waiting for the final exposer. So many think that they have anything to learn, not so, you all learn whatever level you are on. It's a lot to deal with. It's not an easy task but who said it would be. Like many times before, go back to school this time. This time you are in a more advance class. The last two years you have done more serious work then many life times before. You did make a promise to sort and sift to find out what makes what activated, or alive. It's back to the universal law. And you are learning fast. It's not always easy to see the motives behind it all. Some have not got any soul left, controlled by darkness and have lost their free will. Temptations always lead to control. Tested and tried once again and you did pass, as we knew you would.

Love and courage. From TttA

START AGAIN!

It's always good to start afresh. You have a break and then get time to look at the situation again with new eyes. When overdoing things you get out of order in one way or the other. When adversities arise stop and take time out and ask us what and where. Too much is going on behind the scenes for you to be able to make a decision. Stand back and wait for us to give you a sign. Make sure that is us. Holograms and make belief are about more now than before. Courage and help is given every day and you can rest. You will be OK soon. Some days things not planned turn out for the best for all concerned. Only look for today, tomorrow will take care of itself. Carry on with your work and ask for peace and harmony. Your poets are also picking up a lot from all the changes around you. Let the sun warm and calm you and thank us for the clearing and cleaning. You don't have to concern yourself about tomorrow. That is for us. Rest a while then start again. You are learning and growing.

Love and light from TttA

LIVE AND LET LIVE!

The tide is turning and you are feeling all the changes. Don't get carried away with it all. Stay as you are and be a good observer. To act in a different roll will help you to see another side of the coin. The same goes for people. Walk for a minute and two in their shoes and feel what's going on also to get a better idea. What make people act and say what they do? Most of the time they only are hitting out as a reaction to what happen in their life. Still we say leave them to us and we will give you what will be your part to do. Take care not to get involved too much time could easily be spent on cleaning up and untangle it all. Go on with today a little at the time and unwind in between. Your system is so sensitive so you need extra care and protection at present time. It will not be like that forever so stay close to us and we will make sure that you have all you want. Go up higher above it all and get a bird view of your situation.

Blessed be from us all. TttA

ENLIGHTENMENT!

Be grateful for every ray of light on the situation. Remember that all souls have a purpose in your life. Thank all for work done but after send them to us do deal with. All the different paths are there because of all the developments on so many levels. You have seen that a lot lately you did not like how things went but it had to be done. Too much leaching and energy drain. Serious souls need your time and space. We will guide you to when and what. As for the implants you have a way to find out where and when. Remember that we give you the information. That will help you to save many situations and don't let souls that are not aware be. Once again we say let us deal with it. You yourself are doing more than well and you soon will be ready for more evolved situations. In the meantime go ahead with today's work and remember this time is only temporary.

For many it would look like forever. Time is only a human thing, so don't get involved with all that discussions.

Courage and love. TttA

TODAY IS A DAY OF PRAISE!

We are gathered with you today to celebrate a day of peace, joy and calm with health. So much has been sorted and still miracles do happen. Let go today of the residue. It has now served its purpose. New tasks ahead with renewed strength. You did have to get through all that to be able to understand. And leave the past behind. Unease and unrest will stay away from you from this day forward. The meeting of the braves from so long ago will benefit all concern and help you all to understand the nature and your fellow man, you will also get a new trust in the source. It was clear to us what was happening, but you wanted to be sure before acting. So many kinds of interferences made you very cautious. In the silence of the morning you will settle down and renew your strength. That's the price that you have been praying for eons. No more! Enough is enough. Peace and eternal love. Rest in your soul forever.

Amen to that. TttA

GOOD MORNING!

Yes it's a very good morning. Yesterday will benefit you and so many others. It's all a chain reaction to what's going on. One little forgiveness as well as will help to even the balance. That system will get the slate clean and make all communication more pleasant and loving. The divine source of life will fully support and give you all the wisdom that's needed. Today is indeed a new day. The angelic visit was really necessary for your growth and freedom also to connect closer to us. Use colour wisely and play your music that will lift the vibrations in your heart. Start smiling again that will be another beginning to your increasing health. Always check first if spirit is in charge then go on. So many times make believe are playing games. If in doubt do nothing until you are completely sure all is well. This is a new day and you will feel the difference soon. Blessings and love from us all.

Your' loving teachers and friends. TttA

REFRESH AND SMILE AGAIN!

Yes what a good idea. So much clearing and so much were released. Good. That was about time that was done. It's very easy to let things slide or be forgotten. Look at the time when you did something important for spirit and your growth. Try to see what the best time is, in your case.

Everyone have a built in clock so follow what's natural for you. Sometime you can't, because of circumstances, but do the best you can. Stay grounded to be able to see what's going on and stay firmly on the earth. That will also help you to balance things up. Your body is also changing so be patient with it. Rest and enjoy the suns warmth. Not long now before you are feeling yourself again. Testing time was necessary for your future work installed for you. Trust and ask us and all will turn out just fine. Today's keywords are- "Just be and let us". Any other subject can wait.

Loving thoughts and care from us all. TttA

GOOD TIDINGS!

Congratulations you made it! Remember to give thanks to the universe for all the positive happenings. You have now reached another plateau in your life and will advance even faster. The world needs a lot of light workers because of the interference are so great at present. So stay vigilant and stay close to the source were all yours guides' and wisdom comes from. Let the day as from now, you will be very occupied and many will be asking for your input from us. No more blockages and no one can ever do what they have been doing for so long to you. Peace is with you my child of light. Let other do their own thing and when or if they will ask you. Ask us to deal with it and pass on what we say. Blessings are upon you and more protection. Some waters are dangerous and full of rocks. Look up and stay steady, so be the captain of your own ship. Onwards and upwards my dear friend. Amen to that.

Thank you from us all. TttA

OUR FATHER!

My children you are my family and I am another Father God for all you have seen of late and you don't need to concern yourself for not having enough protection or what you need. STOP! You as well as others connected are under the heavenly umbrella. Leave it all to us, you are so independent but it's less now than before. You are truly working on that to ask. My storehouse is full and we want you to understand that's real. My beloved lighthouse workers don't delay what needs to be done. Go ahead in my name and ask. We know your thoughts but we cannot act before you ask. Today's sunshine will engulf and warm you. All that energy will enter your body down in to the very core. We are sending extra strength, balance and love to your connections. All is indeed well with you all. The music will also help you to lift your thoughts to us and the higher realms. Blessings are upon your household and all that belongs to you.

Amen and blessed be. TttA

SORT OUT TIME!

That is what we want you to do now. Once again you are having another look at what to keep and what to give away. New input is waiting for you to make room for. That's a sign that you are changing and growing. Don't stop now you are moving away from old energies and old feelings. That will make you to feel better and detach yourself from that time. Hoarding items or ideas that is no longer useful is no good. Save what you will use and what will make you comfortable. A new time is waiting for you and you don't have to worry anymore. All that you want will appear and more joy will come from the inside. The sun is shining again that will also help you to smile and relax. So much has been in a cocoon for eons. No more time to take the lid off and then you will have a chance to do what you were trained for. The ideas and strength will come as you want. Do your homework today and keep on giving all you feel like replacing.

Blessing and love from us all. TttA

EARLY BIRD!

We know that discipline is increasing in your case, but early in the wintertime makes work a little harder. Well don't be too hard on yourself Warm up and start as soon as you can. Daily routine is always called for and like we have said the work will be done when you do. Your life is unfolding so go with it. New input and more work will come, don't overdo, only one situation at the time. Look after your own time and healing is on-going. Trust us the only safe thing you have in your life many of your so called friends do try but not always succeed to help you. One day that will change. The time is not for you to know. Confusion is still in the air so leave all important decisions for later. A day in the sun will save a lot for most people. Get on with work given for today and you will begin to feel lighter in spirit mind and body Go up again tonight and let the stars guide you on your travel. Disturbed soul will settled down and all will be well again.

Lots of love and joy from TttA

STAY TUNED!

Important messages will be lost otherwise. Let go of being influenced in the physical of the interruptions. Stay clear as much as possible of negative people and entities. Your sensitivity is not an easy task to deal with. You are mixing so much with others so keep your guard up. The trust is building up, but go easy on yourself. Things will be done in time, and time out will also help. Don't despair you are doing the right thing, and will keeping on doing so. We do trust you and are around you but stay close to the source. So much and so many are doing what they can to interrupt your day and night. Ask for a stronger shield and a rain bow veil at all times. This morning you got one more proof that people are doing you harm in two areas. We will see to that it will not happen again. Your work is important and will be hindered if delayed. You know all that, but this is a reminder, for all that's working for the light and their own growth. Keep vigilant and stay tuned.

Courage and love from TttA

REVELATIONS!

Unfolding and opening are the keys for today. You are doing just that. Remember to always guard your body when taking off to another dimension. When you want to go, ask for genuine positive teacher to go with you and bring you back safely. When tired you need to rest and feel that the recharge coming in to your body mind and soul. Protections are of essence and always make sure you have got the most possible kind. Yesterday's meeting was very enlightening. Now you know how much this time was meant to teach you so you can carry on with your work. He will understand in time. Don't ask too much or let him be. If he does not call for your assistance. Time to pay back and time to smile again. You have done so much work so go easy on yourself and others and others like you. You all have a journey to travel further away from your level of understanding. Do not follow some else's speed. And when we suggest stop and pause. You still are in a vulnerable position and we are doing our best to care for you. Trust and rest.

Care and love always. TttA

CALM IN THE STORM!

You as well as others give that thought a chance. Do still only what you feel is right. Today's session was a very big help for you and will benefit all mankind in due course. Now when you finally know why you can let it go. Go on with further work. The big blockage and onslaught was meant to get rid of you. And that was so strong that you started to ask more questions. You also know now what happened for so many thousands of years ago. Well done to receive your new picture. Blessed be. Let the healing take place and unfold the new you don't concern what others will do or say. They have not got any ideas and have been used as puppets. Leave all that to us Tonight we all will be with you as we have promised. The session will still be beneficial for all that attend. Let our love and light show you the way. Guided and lit you will find the path of your goal.

Light and healing with support from TttA

STEADY AS SHE GOES!

Take a step at the time and don't look to far ahead. Too much future is not so good picture. So much will change and so much in every body's life is altering. Take one situation and one day at the time. Mixing and mingling is not the same thing. Do mingle by all means amongst others but do not stay if you are feeling uneasy about it all. To mix people with others might be fine when all parts are compatible, otherwise it will be uneasy and dissatisfaction for many. A sensitive person will have a harder time because of picking up others thoughts and actions. It's best to develop a thick outer shield and a strong cover of a space suit, to be able to see out and have nobody looking in. Beware and stand back if you don't feel 100% right about it all. Ask us for guidance and help will be given. Don't delay the process and feel safe. You are getting the right advice.

Courage to live laugh and love. TttA

LET MY SUN WARM YOU UP AND ALSO MY SON TO HELP YOU TO KEEP IT SO!

That's a thing you need to ponder about. This time of the year you need a lot of extras of all that study and visualisation that picture so you can keep on going. Whatever comes in your work or whatever you see know where your strength is coming from. That's what we mean when we say. Keep the line open and stay close. That's not an order only a reminder from old reliable truth. Nothing is really new only old truth amiable to all mankind in an understandable version. That's way in my days on Earth I spoke in parables for the masses that could not get the message any other way. That's also why I give you tools to operate with and to help you to see what's needed for that soul that comes to you and mostly has tried many other versions and did not get healed. Today will be a revelation day you will be surprised when someone enter I will be there.

Blessings for the day. TttA

GET ON WITH TODAY!

Today is a new day so yesterday's work is done and today you are carry on next on the next page of your life. To build a strong character is not easy but that's the way you can grow and teach others how they can walk on their path. Still we say don't give out before we have told you if the situations called for advance sorting, give it to us to finish off. We also are reminding you about don't give beef to a baby. Many cannot see where they are and how much they can digest and also let us put the seeds in to their spirit when or who to see. The advancement of the soul is to be gradually understood and accepted. Its one thing to read the truth in a book or hear it from a teacher another thing is to fully grasp the whole picture. Most do that in stages so it can be connected and the line of the communication will be fully opened up. It's very important that you don't take it for granted or likely to with your advancement. The higher you go the more you need to do.

Blessings from TttA

WELL DONE!

Let today be a day of joy work and organizing. You know what that will make in time and energy saving. Put a little spark in your own life and someone else's. That will also ignite the flame of love and light. This time of the year when so many are freezing and not feeling the warmth of your sun and the son of God. Human conditions are not the best just now but it will change later. In the meantime stay close to the source and meditate and surrender. The will of the father is taken care of it all so relax and listen in. Support each other and let all of you develop and show your talents and true potential. You all have them so work and show others that was what given to you from birth. The abilities were given to you to help yourself and others to grow. Don't compare talents and gifts. Encourage and support will work much better. Praise is another way to encourage to awaken spirit mind and body. These words are given to you all so you know that is fine from the universal wisdom and love. We all are behind you and always will be.

Your support team. TttA

CONNECT AND ENJOY!

Remember the old times and old good feelings. It was a lot of them then. To learn from them and situations was the lesson. Don't take for granted the good times but use them to restore and help your fellow man. Your experiences have taught you how to survive and start again after a down fall. Anything is possible. Miracles still happen when it's meant to be there to show you there is a miracle and there is a father in heaven. So many times the Lord's Prayer has been said but not fully understood. Well now you have of late got a new picture of the meaning. Thank you for open your mind and heart and connect your spirit with ours. The line is getting stronger and not so easy blowing in the wind. As we have told you many times only bend and do not break. It's natural for all to feel different at times but that's for you to understand and coming alive from. Let today be a time of nurturing and joy. Little bell ringing's and happy thoughts will make your day much more pleasant.

Blessed be from TttA

TODAY IS A SUNNY DAY!

Let my son and my sun warm you up once more. This time of the day you all need to look at extra, light candles incense and you will get extra energy. That is only a little reminder how to best survive and grow in this cool season. That is to change so in the waiting time you will do what's best for today. To be flexible is still good. You needed a little reminder how much how many lives are entangled with others and how many different levels you are dealing with. Also think how much is going around you. That's because more people are looking at the happenings of their own lives and they want to know why and when. The timing is very much of importance as you already know about father time and Mother Nature. Keep in mind what and when. Take notice of all the signs we are giving you and help you with your decisions. First stay calm and empty out so you have room for more input and knowledge that you will need for your work. The supply is there so you only have to ask. Once again today is a reminder about old truth.

Love and laughter from TttA

SUNRISE!

Enjoy the new start of the day and it's a new day. Yesterday's work has been done so be thankful it turned out as it did. You did ask for our input so it was dealt with for the best. The two ladies will start to feel the benefit today. Maybe they don't understood yet, but it does not matter. The saving and the enlightenment of souls is important so let us do our work and for you to do yours. You are still being trained for more advanced work, so get your own work in order. Empty out and be ready to receive more fresh thoughts. We have been with you now for a long time and it is a very strong bond. It was necessary to train you in more than one area at the same time. As we say you are rising up from your experiences and you will get higher still. Leave any ego thoughts behind and see the purpose in the way it's happening. Today you will be shown a fuller picture. The unfolding time is here and it will teach you once again how complex situations can be. Past lives with past happenings will influence next life. Enjoy and take time out.

Blessings from us all. TttA

A DAY OF REMEMBRANCE!

My child you do have a lot of interesting events to remember. So much to learn from and so many situations to look at. All people are on a quest and some on a long journey, others only a very short time. All the timing is for us to deal with and for you to follow through. Look at life as a learning school. You don't always advance to a higher level if not your souls go back and check where you have to relearn and act in a clearer way so no misunderstandings will occur. You could also get your wires crossed when not focusing enough. Stay still and wait if the way is not open yet. All the parts need to be synchronized to work together for a good result. So many want to work for themselves or don't like to ask. That's pride and the self which all of you are dealing with. Ponder on that truth for a while. Time is of essence and don't hurry anyone or anything.

Courage and love from us all. TttA

THE TRUTH IS SIMPLY WONDERFUL!

To look at the truth and discover the picture of simplicity and wonder is indeed a fortunate thought. The way you will discover will open to you, and one chapter at a time will reveal what you want to know and when. Trust and smile throughout the storm, wind and rain. It's all there for a purpose and when it occurs you might not know why but in time when fitted in to place you will fully see what was going on. Thank us, your teachers, patiently staying by and waiting to assist you about different levels of understanding for your growth and for you to give to others. Take care not to overdo anything and forgive yourself for not always doing what was required of you. It was all another test. Let go of all thoughts to be perfect, no one is but you will work again and again to be able to see what area you need to work on. You already know most of that but it's not easy for you. Keep on trying support and laughter. More tomorrow. Have a good day all in the name of the light.

Thank you! TttA

TRUST AND WISDOM!

Thus two words will help you to handle your life. Trusting the source and give you all the wisdom that you need and want for your work and life. Understand and use thus two words for your growth strength and wisdom. By now you will see a change in your thinking due to more positive input from new connections that we have sent to you. You really don't know all the support and work been done without your knowledge. You did sense something was going on for your faith to be tested. We could not tell you. Soon you will see more of the pattern that makes your work and future work possible. Therefore we say again anything is possible for the ones that work, trust and believe that miracles can happen and will. So let the day unfold as it may. Back to the time when you learned, teach and connected. That's still very possible. You are doing just that without noticing many times. Stay on track and let tonight be another connection time. We are leading them to you so open up your home and sanctuary for them and us. We know that all will be for the best for you and for us.

Blessed be TttA

INFLOW AND OUTFLOW!

So much depends where you are getting your input from, and where does it go? Don't think for a moment that you are doing that on your own. We are guiding you to your goal and in turn you are guiding others. That comes to your sanctuary. We know by now how you are connected and your work on Earth this time is taken very seriously. So much time has not been used at the best of values. At present time you are doing more than before because you are advancing and doing your own home work. Keep on doing just that until further notice. We are with you at all times now. So souls that come to you feel that and want to know what to do to get it. Your soul is now in charge so let others do their part. Your spirit journey is coming along with good contacts and valuable support. Today will also tell a story from the past and explain today's happenings. Let us do the thinking.

Lots of loving, wisdom and light. TttA

LIGHT ONE MORE LIGHT TODAY!

Let my light comfort and cheer you today and always. The light and love will serve you well and help many others that are coming on to your path. Extra warmth will be needed because of the shift. That will settle down. The rest of the winter will be slightly warmer for this time.

All others areas will also be changeable for a time but that has to do with other clearings and situations. Take care of all that comes to you but only your part in site and let us do the work on a deeper level. Everyone has their part to do and still let us know who and where to strengthen our bonds. We already know what the pattern is and keep on giving and repeating giving you practical examples. You will never forget our principles. Many do not understand that it takes time to absorb the truth of our teachings. Today is another day of inside opportunities. Colour light and incense with love will keep you going always through your life. Maybe a little changes here or there. Still take a day at a time loving and lighting you and some else's day.

Thank you. TttA

ENERGY INPUT!

Look at where you get your energy from. Always check how it feels like when being recharged. In time you will know in an instant what's going on. Also look at people's eyes including pets. Do they meet yours in comfort and recognition or avoiding the contact. The whole person will tell you about positive and negative feelings plus at times you can smell an unpleasant odour. When you do detach stay clear. It's not a physical expression only what's inside them comes out in a very unpleasant odour in a very offensive sulphur smell. All of that information is a sign what's going on and for all to take notice of. Let us know in details the more specific you are the better. Things will move and you are on the right track. Carry on as you are a little time for yourself as well as others. Love yourself as you are, trying to improve your situation with our help. Never ever give up. Trials will come for most of you, but see them as tests. After all you are still human with human feelings and actions.

Love and courage from us all. TttA

ENJOY THE HEAT FROM THE SOURCE!

Please do. And take in all energy that we send you with all our eternal love and we are doing our best to make all things as easy as possible for your growth and survival. Think and give us a little more time, consideration and joy. It's hard this time of the year, but it will not last for long. In the meantime go easy on all living things. All that have life-force and a spark of the creator will live and prosper. Today is a working day again. Only do a little at a time. Take time out and just be. We do understand how much you have against you ask us still to deal with it, as you only know a part of it. Remember also to leave all deeper entangles cases to us. Lately you have been challenged and many are complicated It's only to remind you about life, and how complex humans are. Some only go on their merry go round forever and others finally start to think. All it is only hypnotic or some form of main programming. Alert signals when feeling that, STOP and ask us. Detach and stay clear.

Love and cheers from TttA

LET LOVE CONQUER!

Remember to ask for more love. You all are being tested, and need to use eternal love as a force to sort out and come across the bridge for the best way possible for everyone's best solution. The hardest part is to see and listen to the answers from all your teachers from the past. Many eons ago and still with you. That is something to appreciate for ever. Don't let others so called thoughts give your day a grey feeling. Never ever go with others dread or negativity. Make a break and go to the light, at the same time send all others to us. They all have their own lessons to learn, and their own quandary, and back to the source. Have compassion but don't get involved. Let your love shine from the top of the hill and beware of side tracks and clowns. They are not what they seem to be. Always look inside the person and then find out what the course of it is. Never judge another or you for anything only learn from it.

Blessed be from TttA

LOVE EACH OTHER!

To let my love and light enlighten and warm your hearts and mind. The universal light and wisdom will also support your ideas and give you energy and the will to work and have compassion for others. You all need that help especially under these cold winter days. Extra surprises and a little more care will soon change all that. The different needs for different levels are quite clear but still ask us when and how. Also a good communication between us and you also between other souls that come to you and are searching for the truth. Remember that the truth will only be told at the level they understand at the moment. Later more when they are ready. It's no good to push any truth and wisdom that will fall on stony ground. Take a spell on your plateau, when rested climb up again. You can see the pattern and you are better able to follow true. The time will soon come for better conditions and better acceptable exchanges. Keep your spirit up and think happy thoughts and love yourself as much as you can. Keep on trying never giving up.

Love and cheers from us all. TttA

UNFOLDING TIME!

Let this time be used as an unfolding and sort out time. So many have so much buried for such a long time ago so it has been left to fester. Now is the time to slowly look and find a solution to it all. The best way you can do it is to surrender to us, one case at the time. So much grief and so many broken hearts. Most of all wounded souls that also need to feel joy and peace once again. So many think they own another person or control emotions and actions of someone else. That is a crime against spirit and should not be ignored. Ask for a suitable solution without making other decisions. Let go of the world's ideas of what should be done and when. It was said so many times. It is not done these days. But that is not really what has happened. No one would stand up for themselves because of fear and pride. Rather suffer in privacy. Yesterday you did have a chance to see close up- what was someone's back ground and the beginning of a period of uncertainly with complication to follow. Stand by and listen with compassion and give your time.

Blessed be TttA

GOOD WORK TODAY!

Once again you have followed through what we ask you to do. It was important that you dealt with one case at a time. That went very well. So many different levels of souls and so many degrees of understanding. Don't look at them all at once. Study the pattern in them all and learn to remember what you see hear and smell of universal wisdom we trust you with more work now. Intricate and involved it might seem at first. As you were growing you were told about deeper questions and situations. Today you have experienced 3 different levels of attitude to come yet. All day it is a reminder from the past days and old truth. Tomorrow it will be a study day again. The world is confused and hungry for soul food and mostly they forget to fill up their tanks and running on empty. That's a good picture to keep in mind using a parable. Some only can remember a picture not too many spoken words. That's fine. Whatever it might be at the time suitable ask us. Once again thank you for working for us and the source.

Love and wisdom from TttA

LATE AGAIN!

We have been close to you now for a long time.so we can tell when you are going to be late. Look at another pattern. Go easy after a day with mixed happenings. Well now you will get your wish once again you are doing your very best to accomplish the tasks that you have been given. Some still are trying very hard to disrupt you, or take your energy. Worst when they disregard help, wisdom and knowledge from us, through you. Leave them all to us. You know how often you have done your very best and got a negative response. That will show you were they are and how little they know. By your actions you will feel how much is accepted and passed on through you. Ponder on that thought and understand who is talking to you and from were. Let our light go before you and let our wisdom make you grow and in turn you pass on to others to help them also to link in to us.

Blessings be upon you and all others that come in contact with you. From TttA

WORK AND REST!

Let today unfold in a natural way. When you don't know all of it, wait and leave situations to be explained and sorted. Go up to us still at night, as many times you need that time out and you will know why later. Complications and interference have been rearing their ugly heads of late. That was to be expected as after all you are being challenged most days. This morning you got one more proof of our support and work. The environment support system, is also working now. You did see the changes from a neighbour. Use caution about the other lady. She wants some of your energy, so she is trying to disturb you by her actions. It's two of her as well as the A case. Your four years has gone for the clearing to occur so it was an involved situation. Now you can understand why it has taken so long to sort out. You did learn a lot from it though. The sun will help to just to warm you up and just be, as it will get lighter outside so will you feel a breeze of life and joy coming over you. Some human conditions are still to be resolved when its ready and all involved have learnt and look at the facts. Strength and wisdom for your highest good.

Love and light TttA

STOP AND START AGAIN!

Remember when the situations call for stop or recharge and re think, do so. Lately that has been happening. The water people and weather have been doing just that. It's a reason for the season. The changes and the new systems are being looked at. Don't be surprised when it will happen again. Still we say go ahead with today's work. We will see to it that you are protected and not misused. The cold weather will also kill off any undesirable bugs. You are not cut off, only protected, so you can do your work undisturbed. Trust that the pattern of your life is unfolding satisfactory. Once again leave it us to sort out. Also the new neighbour will be of resistance not hindrance. All supporting you now from now on and we are giving you extra help also. Others that disturb you or stun you will also know all about it. Go ahead, and the sun will keep you warm and flexible. As you advance so will the pressure to stop you. It's really in your favour. Ask for a new invisible tool for new workload.

Protection and joy from TttA

ASK AND YOU WILL RECEIVE!

That's the only time promise we give you. Still we say be careful what you do ask for to specify and listen in. We are listening to you all in all communications and cooperation's in actions. The same goes for the spiritual growth. The link between two souls and the same goes for linking in with us. Be an observer and study actions and reactions on people animals and all living things. Today once again you got a clear picture of lives situations that gave some a scared life. That has to look and become a new tissues and balm comes with new eternal love and real honesty. To injure one soul you injure many others to come. Learning how things oscillate when not getting sorted or understood. Too many get side tracked or do not fully understand the motive behind the other people's actions. Stay an onlooker and be a good observer. To help,guide many in the future, and history often repeat itself, so look learn and use your nose to smell alterations and advantages on the scale of growth and connections of the level of wisdom.

Love and light to all students. TttA

CLAIM MORE!

Remember a long time ago that that you did not understand a situation. We ask you to claim understanding then and you got it. That is a reminder of the law of supplies.

Give away something when the energy has gone stagnant and new life comes in to you as we promised you that to be true. So pass it on to others. They might already have practiced but forgotten a long time ago. Repetition is the key to wisdom. That's an old saying but try it is working for you. Don't repeat old mistakes though, you learn from them. Nothing is a waste so look at it as a learning curve. Yesterday's event worked out well you got clear in your mind what was going on. That was a practical lesson another from the visit from the south unexplained but important. The lesson was to act as a link once again. The different levels of souls that we send to your door are all as it should be. You still are a bridge worker activator and healer. Go ahead with your book and cooperate.

Light, love and joy from TttA

TIME OUT TO REJOICE!

Today you have worked hard again to do your part of the work. You don't need to do any more work today. Unwind and enjoy! We will see to it that you do. It's better to have a break often so you can work and do what you want when the need is there. The sun is shining again after the refreshing rain last night. The meditation proved to be rewarding and at times you still wonder who will come and what will take place, but that is natural. Leave it to us what to do what's needed. With the changes around you it will ease for your life. Less tension for all. New life will come soon so wait and let us send the best suitable person. It has been a big test, but you did learn from the unfolding of your other connections what is on-going. The new book is now half way with one part. We will support you and whoever is working with you. The unblocking in all other areas is under way. Your group is remodelling itself. Be patient and be an observer. We know that will working out for the best. Help for all is given.

Loving support from TttA

STOP AND RECHARGE!

Today many have to stop and rethink what you are doing. No one or nothing can keep going on empty. Tender loving care and rest with relaxation is a start. A strong healthy refill is the fastest and best way. You all know where to go and to whom but quite often humans go to many other people and places to look for a solution. That is a part of the human mind and pre-programming. Hypnotic influences have played a big part in it all and so much is also controlled by negative thinking and dark thoughts. The wrong teachers and the media are also playing a big part. My children always stay firm, steady and wise. That is not an order only the best suggestion we can offer you. Support and take care of each other. All of you should try a little harder to give trust love and support to each other.

The darkness is trying it's very best to split the light and minds of so many. Detach and retreat in to your own space.

Love and eternal support from TttA

BLESSINGS FOR YOUR WORK!

It's a good thing to be blessed. That will increase your workload and spread light in to many places. You know that the backup system is very important so let us know when you need some. The whole system of yours has been waiting to emerge in to a better more focused and strong and in one unit. Don't delay further actions to improve your life. You have been very patient and there have been so many tests. They all were necessary for your initiation. Some still think they know you, detach from the hangers on and leeches. They can easily learn to do their own homework. By all means start them on their own journey. As you are an activator it will work fast. Today is another workday. There are many that would do with a little more discipline. Be happy with your work and yourself. You have come through another face and chapter. Enjoy today and cheer others up also.

Starbright –starlight will follow you all the way. TttA

ONCE AGAIN YOU HAVE UNDERSTOOD!

My child of light you have had a hard time to connect situations and souls, and also to recognise who is who. No more- you have a new way to check and that was important for your work. Don't think that the work you did was not quite right or on target. It's has taken a lot of focusing and detachment to be able to see. Stay positive and trust that we still have all in hand. The opposition knows fully well how it would be if you were not on this Earth anymore. Tough is it not? You did know about it all, and we are still there with you. Yesterday is now gone and it turned better to the end. The conditions were not suitable for you, but you did manage to do it all. Today is another day and you will see proof once more again. The two females today have their own story to tell. You will be an observer and check in with us. Don't judge, get emotional or negative about anything. It will not serve any purpose or the Cause. Go on in our peace and remember it's a new day. Treat it as such.

Blessings and warmth from TttA

DETACH AND STAND BACK!

When you have done so you will see the full picture and get a clear view. So many of late have appeared to be interested in your work and they are doing all the right things. If not genuine the bubble will burst one day. The others are honest and really looking for the truth. All the different souls that come will have a motive. That is for you to work out when you think all is done. Check with us and we will tell you. Today you did get proof once more. Look at the signs we sent to you. Don't concern yourself with little crazy interferences that have only to disrupt and disturb you and once more it did not work. We have now put extra protection around you and we are guarding your connections with a sharp eye. You did find out a little more as to who is who, and that's good. Still deal with them as you have been asked to do. Stay firm and positive and you will get all the support and help you want. Tonight a few more areas get sorted out. Where they are and who they are.

Blessings to all. TttA

REFRESH AND ENJOY!

It's good to be able to do just that. To change colour or alter something makes a change of energy. At times you only have to smell the roses or do something positive for someone. Very many want to be able to do just that but they have gone away from making lovely interactions. Exchange of energy and thoughts of up lifting nature is also of big value. Focus on one kind of love every day and it will make ripple on the surface of the water. Later on it will go deeper and look at other issues. When the time is under control of divine timing all will fit in and help and sort out and guide and help you to make the right choices under your travel to time and space. Last night's input was beneficial for all. Activate and energise all that's needed. Go along your path and travel on your journey. Don't ever walk on some else's path. That would not benefit you or them. Think and feel when you know the time is, time to act. Let us give you the thought pattern and help with our guiding light.

Our blessings be upon you. TttA

BLESSINGS TO ALL!

Let our blessings and joy come in to your soul. In to the very core of your love and strength to enrich you and spread hope to all. My care is now for all of you that work for the light. It's not for you to say or think who is who. Leave all that to us. We are the only once that knows and can see all. My beloved children you are getting all help you will require for your part of the work for the eternal source. Everyone has talents so use them. When you do, progress will follow. Otherwise it will turn into stagnation. And no further growth. Today will be an inspiring day. So much to catch up on and deal with, an area long forgotten about. That will heal you and help you to understand why. So many lifetimes has gone so it has taken time to unfold. Let it all come to fruition. That will enrich your life and others. Still understand that you all are instruments playing in the same orchestra. Enjoy today and relax in between all the work you are doing with your new book.

Light and wisdom on your path from TttA

OPEN UP TO THE JOY AND HEALING!

Empty out so we can refill your spirit mind and body. It's all on-going and circulating as we have said so many times. No stagnation over and over so many times. Still take in and try to understand what is the system and who is taken so long time. Let's talk about it. Time is manmade and eternal time is for us and it comes from the father. Remember that the father and I are one and the same. The father son and Holy Spirit is a part of the same unit. They all are activated when one is all are. The God spark is in all of you. Down on Earth you call it the life force, living in all created beings. Without that nothing could live. When gone it was sent back to the source. Yesterday was a healing and working day. To be able to assist and work with others is indeed a blessed gift. At times you don't understand or remember other lifetimes but we have it all in the book of life. Lessons learned is good but don't stop there. Keep on going and be glad that you are able to. Enjoy what you can do and do something for someone every day.

Blessings and love from TttA

PREPARING TIME!

That is what we ask you to do. Prepare and sort out who or what to keep. Let us give you the basic truth and then work on the other small parts. That is to say get in to order. Discard whatever is not needed and store other practical objects for further use. It will also save time later on. Time is energy so treat is as such by looking how you spend your energy. Have time out and have discipline, but don't overdo anything. It could turn out to an obsession. That would turn in to a controlled situation. Back to balance again. All interested in spiritual growth would greatly benefit from basic ground rules. The main thing is to do your homework and study with a good teacher and helpful groups. Study behaviour and time into feelings. It's got to do with law of spirit and the universal teachings. Stay working as you are the work is getting done in just the right time. The people that need to read your books are appearing on the horizon. The law of supply is operating as good as ever.

Light love and laughter from TttA

SORTING AND SIFTING!

That is what we want you to look at today. You have done just that for quite a while now so carry on. Memories are sometimes hard to get rid of. Healing is given every day and mostly through the night. One day you will feel fantastic. Keep on with your exercises and regimes. Your whole body has been through so many changes It's been quite hard at times but you are benefitting from all that now and later better still. No one can fully understand how much work is involved getting the books out but it is for the good of all mankind. You are not doing it for you it's for all that are searching for the truth. It has helped you, and it will keep on guiding many for times to come. Today will tell a story and tonight and you will see more who is who. We are there and you asked for all to be cleared before they come to you. We check with you at all times. Your home has become a station once more for us to use as we see it. Keep on with your writing and we will send more work to you. The blockage is being re moved.

Eternal love and light from the source TttA.

LOOK BEHIND THE MASK!

Once again I say it's not enough to look at the cover and search for the deeper truth. Many times it's covered up to hide or confuse the issues. Peel off all the covers and see what lies behind so you can see into the very core is indeed a big task. Ponder on that truth until it sinks in to your very soul. Let today's events and clearing out be to a big blessing. Indeed it was necessary to clean up behind the wall and get a fresh start. The renewal of energy was very important for all concern. Take it as it was meant. You will have a clear input after the blockage has been taken away. The test was flexible and calm whatever the moment will bring you. Look at the visitors in the same way. They all did what was best for you, so be grateful for. For the exchanges and learn from them. If and when you don't understand, ask for an explanation and always clean up from the inside first. Give thanks to the supplier of all wisdom health and joy.

RESTORE AFTER THE POSITIVE ACTIONS!

Remember the law of cause and effect. What you sow you will reap. Good thoughts and good actions will come back to you 10 times over. Let go after the last sad feelings as happiness is knocking at the door. It will not enter before all past, not wanted ideas and thoughts have vanished. Today is another day of communications and another step upwards. Still we say take time out between "jobs". So much more will be done when you starting a fresh. The same after a good night's sleep, you will get a fresh outlook and your energy will extend to a fat bigger circle. The mist outside will clear as well as the one inside some peoples mind. All can see but not all can accept the picture. In time they will see what's going on and get a better prospective of events in their life. Gods speed with the work on your plate today. The practical side also needs attention. All our love, blessings and health for you and yours.

Blessings as always. TttA

SUNNY RAYS!

Well now that is exactly what you all need. The sun will bring out all the energy that you all need. The life force is needed to get a top up. Wintertime is not easy in your land. We do know how cold and damp it gets many times. Ask for a speedup of the changes.so one more time will do it. Keep us close to you and relax so you can operate so much faster. The warmer times are coming so keep that in mind as the sun return once more to you. Really it's the Earth turning around in its' orbit. Enjoy the positive changes and let the feeling go in your heart and warm up the feelings from the past. Forgiven and released make the whole body healthier. It's always a reaction in the body cells and the chemicals when events occur. Still remember to talk to your body and send it love and light. All the parts of your body are living cells and have feelings. So hate and love are very strong activators of disease or health. Your choice!

Wisdom and light with love from TttA

DEW DROPS!

Blessed be to those who can feel the dew drops on the very core of their soul. That will soothe and refresh you. So many souls has been wounded and scared through so many life times. To feel the small dewdrops coming in to the core, to heal and help you to live again. The healing in very soft and nurturing way is many times the best. Too much or too soon, would be too much for many. Gently doe's it. Enjoy the thought and possibility it's working and miracles still happen. Rest assured that is our holy promise. Rely on us first of all. People are helping but only when they are guided by the universal love and have a commitment to work for the light for ever. You of all people will understand what that' all about. So many do try, but are not committed. To them we say try again, it's never too late to have another chance and to fully understand what is the purpose to it all. Blessed are the meek and lowly. Blessed be to my beloved children. I am your father in more than one way.

Always yours TttA

ENERGY BLESSINGS!

Once again we are sending you energy blessings to all that it and to enhance your whole system's much has been used up so it is wise to get fresh input once more. Fresh eternal energy will do that but remember to empty out every time. Stale energy does not help or advance anyone. Fresh and clean water and recharging outside when possible. The sun will activate your spirit mind and body. It is all working as one unit, but at times one gets neglected. When that happens look at the unfilled areas and spend time to get in in balance again. Unity is very important for your life and work. Discipline and focus is as well. To live in your dimension will test and make you able to handle others and yourself. Lately so many unanswered questions has come through your door one way or the other. We send them to you so you can get practise and learn how to deal with different soul development. Again more will come, ask us to stand by and guide you. Thank you for carry on as much as you are.

Blessings from TttA

KEEP ON COMING ALIVE!

Carry on advancing and teach others that is a good way to inner peace and growth. Remember to do the learning in your speed and understanding. You all are in different levels and knowledge, so don't compare or copy that would not be to your benefit. Be an observer and study that will aid you and be what you were meant to be. And still you respect others opinions. That does not mean to accept or believe. The lessons you all are facing are for the individual and that way you can't mix path ways with somebody else.

Still we say don't tell or order before you get the OK from us. If someone feels pushed they will rebel or stop in their search for a while. Natural unfolding is the most advisable for all. As you have noticed the sun returning, rather the moving in to more light. There will also be more love from the universal source. Be patient and let us guide you through storm or calm whatever comes. If you don't feel or hear anything, wait and that is a sign that you are in transit or that all conditions are not yet sorted.

Happy days are here again from TttA

LOVE AND LIGHT TO ALL!

Let our love and light show you the way and lighten up your life. Whatever you are and who you all want and need more of just that. A fresh input of something positive is very wise at this time, more now than before you are living in changing times, my friends of the light. Stay close to your source and very steady. When you are tired rest, you can't run on empty. No one or nothing will function in that situation. Refill by having time out and do smile more. Life was not meant to be serious, but people are putting so much value of having to do everything right. In some one's eyes. Let go of that idea, you need to go to the father and ask what 'right in someone's eyes. Let go of that idea, advice is always good, but ask from the positive source. We know so do you most of the time, so keep on going on with your discipline. Order is good to save time and energy, you know all that. But this is a reminder. It's so easy to forget when dealing with so many different levels of dimensions. Have a sense when needed and a fresh start again.

Courage and laughter from TttA

CLEAR SKY!

Go out and look at the sky. How many times have you seen the changes and colours shifting in a very short time? So it is with the miracles, they could happen in an instant. Expect it to come and it will. Faith and trust together with a daily input from us will get you towards your goal. Forever learning growing and understanding what life is all about. Also when you are close to something or someone you are unable to see what's going on. Stand back and open up your windows of the soul. Let us clear the view so nothing or nobody stands in your way. It could also be spirit pollutions that clouds you in, so you not able to see. Because you are in a transmission period and not ready for move along. That's why you are asked to do your homework and prepare the ground. Then we can plant and help you to nurture your ground. The same goes for a thing that lives. All of your situations will be sorted. In the divine timing..

Love laughter and light. TttA

FRESH WIND IN YOUR SAILS!

Remember to wait until everything is still and calm. If and when you need to sail out to sea ask for a breeze in your sails to get you moving out further. The tools are always there, so use them. Different tools for different al, clear and encourage you all. Human understanding needs to get the universal wisdom from our teachers. It's all about linking in and receiving. Keep an eye on stale energy. Air it out by changing and turning over objects and thoughts. Forever sorting out and looking at where things are is to get an order in to your life. Don't neglect your time with us. Timing at present is "out". It's looking like a chain reaction or ripples on the surface. Also there is a sign of life underneath, what you don't see at first. Then you will wait once more to use your eyes to penetrate deeper down and then you are able to see what the situation is. Remember your thoughts and actions also have a ripple effect. Let the day be a blessing for some and help for others. Remember we are sending you the souls that want to link up.

Joy and wisdom from TttA

DISCOVERING TIME!

To see and unearth is to discover what lies beneath. After you will spend less time to search and understand the puzzle of life. To try to solve that on your own would indeed be very foolish. You are with many other connected light workers links in a chain for the good of all mankind. When one link breaks the other the other will not operate strongly until a new link has been put in place. It would be a load on for the break. Outworn or not enough faith and trust to name a few. That's why you need to keep vigilant steady and faithful to the source. We are guarding all light workers for the onslaught is grate now before the big shift before another movement. Is about to occur once again. We have to do that slowly to save the human bodies to be able to take the changes into new energies. The human cells are also feeling the effect of the alterations. Still we say have balance as much as possible. Do your best and we will do the rest?

Joy and health to all. TttA

ORDER!

That is a very good clear advice for today. Time and energy will be needed in other areas soon so you have done your tidy up work. That is to clear your slate up so you can spend more time on your work. It's no good to start from the outside. You most go in to the core and see what's needed to be redone or refreshed. After that you can build your tower of strength and a strong fort for further protection also a safe haven for wondering souls. As you already know you are a part of the army of the eternal force work on Earth. It will be a big challenge and a mighty test. Many of your connections will try to alter be sway or even betray, but it will not work. You already know that but we keep on reminding you, so that will reassure you that all is in working order. Let the work and energy flow in your life also keep an unblocked channel. Empty out and receive fresh input. A reminder for you to pass on to others for their support on their journey.

Cheers and love. TttA

PEACE TO ALL!

Universes are always ready to give out goodness love and peace in full measure. You only have to ask and empty out. The old pattern is no longer useful so go higher still to learn more. Go out and up in even wider circles and let the light and love go with you. To aid enjoy and love all. Be wise and think upon this truth. It's really simple but most theology makes it so complex and off putting. So many get disheartened or go along for the sake of it all. That's not honest to your spirit and it will not be a help to your growth. Which is the most important area of your system? First get right with your spirit than all other part will follow. Let my spirit be inside you and lighten up your life and life force. Go deeper still today. You are now better equipped for the next rung in your ladder. Work is always growth in one area or the other. Give yourself time to digest what's going on. Blessings are upon you and yours for today.

Light and love. TttA

TO WAIT IS NOT TIME WASTED!

To be able to do things in the right time is not easy, but the result is better if you do. Listen and let the divine timing be in charge. You might be ready but others are not, so wait. You now have studied that for a few years so keep on practising again and again. Leave this entire situation to work out. Yours is to do your part as you have been trained to do as you have many times called it. Father time is more real than you know. Your father and mine are one and the same. That is what we meant when you say our father in the very well-known prayer Trust that is so; we gave this word for a very special and for you humans to be able to focus to work with our love and support. Put all your positive energy in to your work we refill you after every work signed by us. A little at the time and as you go along. You get faster and being able to receive more and deeper more involved situations. Just as you are going to spirit school learning and advancing. Onwards and upwards.

Joy and support TttA

COME ALIVE!

Yes my beloved children, you are waking up and therefore coming alive. See it as a circle of life. Rest and recharge and then be ready to bloom. The same as the plants and trees in your garden. It all has its season and timing is also involved. The natural way is still the best. Nothing of spiritual growth can be activated if being forced. Ask for divine timing and let us do the sorting. So many souls are in distress because of the shifts and changes. You do know all of that, but we are giving you a timely reminder. Repetition is good many times so you can put in to a deeper level. The deeper you go the deeper the understanding will be. Let our wisdom be of good help and enlightenment for you and your work. Last night was a very good interaction. All joined in and the hope was there to light the flame of spirit. Many have just little ambers glowing for a long time until they are ready to come alive. It needs thoughts, love and light to be able to see what's going on. The flame from us is joining in with yours.

Eternal love. TttA

LOOK AT THE CHANGES!

See what's going on and let others know how to change and alter so much and enhance the energies by replacing or altering here and there. Look again if any and specifically when it does not feel or look right. You would know about all that. Does the environment inside and out present you? Also as you alter your surroundings also alters habits, choice and tastes. Be an observer and keep a close eye on actions and reactions of yourself and others. We also are reminding you about our teachings and to rely on old truth. From today you are free once more. Free from negative interruptions and we can get closer to you. It's pleasing to know who you are listening to and you are getting our signals faster. Still we say don't get vulnerable and when you feel that situations are coming along-beware of your thought patterns and who is coming to your door. Today will bring good tidings and news about queries that you have been wondering about. Enjoy the fresh breeze and all that comes with it.

Blessings and warmth from all of us. TttA

BE THE JOY OF LIFE!

Be just that for yourself and for someone else today. So much joy and health will come out and enhance your life. When joy is not present so many dull thoughts and actions will happen. Go ahead today and enjoy something new and unexpected. Ask for new ways and approach to life. When a solution or a feeling has lost its spark, stop and look what is missing. Ask us for input and follow through. All of the human forms of life are so complex, so be specific. Let the early hours show you what where and how. It's so easy to just go along at the level you are at present, that could very well be a trap for the work to stop or deter you. Don't listen do something else and focus on the keys given today. The miracle will happen and many of you will concur. The last few miles before the goal will tell the story. Go straight ahead and you will get there faster. My sun and my son will support and aid your journey. Relax restore and regain from the source. Your knowledge is increasing and also your outlook is brighter. Thank you for very helpful assistance.

Joy once more. TttA

CHEERING AND SHARING!

That's a good start for the day; you also first do the clearing of the situations. Let go of which way, only do what's for the day. Don't organize too much in one day. Let us do and sort it all out. The timing comes in to it again, so wait is the best when we say so go ahead also applies for the same reason. It's to do with order, and you know that by now. Also a reminder to operate in balance. When things or people do not come when promised the timing is out, so go back to us and ask what next on the agenda. Stay flexible and cheerful. Still a little longer. As the sun is returning or rather the earth, you are getting more light, so send some in to your soul. Your insides are more in need of love and light. That is why we always work from the inside. Go out and spread the word to all we say or have sent to your door. No one comes to you as a coincidence. It's all planned by us. Your group rather ours will increase and the word will spread. Blessings are upon you.

Love and cheers from TttA

WHERE AND HOW!

Where and how was around you this morning. Time was changed again. Well we could see it coming. Let us know in time before the next situation that's needing alteration. Momentary you are distracted and holding back until you are focused and that you have the right situation. That is good to check as you now are calmer and better focused. You need to go easy at times and check to see what's going on and when to move. Testing time will help you to recognise all the signals on your map to follow. Act only when all thought forms are clear and it feels right. You have now carried out many more tasks it's only by trusting and learning from us. Never forget that you still a student and have a lot more of learning to do yet. You still see some miracles happening every day. So that will empower your faith and trust. Nature is waking up so enjoy the new life and it will help you to see colours and shapes more clearly. Forever stay with us to connect and learn.

Supporting thoughts from TttA

REMEMBER YOUR SPIRIT!

Let no one distract or impede you when you do your spirit work, many will try as you so well know but will not succeed. As the sun now gets up sooner on your horizon remind yourself about your soaring spirit. The connection is getting stronger and faster, you have been working on focus and discipline so now you can get through all that and aid others to connect with stronger cords and protected once. The negative side has also seen what's going on so they are having more difficult times to interfere. Send them all to the light and we will deal with them according to the universal law. As your garden is becoming more colourful and the growth is very obvious you will feel the life force enhancing your whole body where the Christ light now lives and help you to do your work for us. See the big picture and do your part still stands. Listen to the birds and the bees they also are telling you a story. All living things are made for you to communicate with. And give you a signal from us. Blessings for all that are helping you to go ahead with your light work.

We are sending them extra love and care. TttA

FIND OUT!

Let your sharp eyes find the missing pieces in your life's puzzles. When you do your life is going to be plain and easier to understand. Too close to a situation and you will not see and not observe too much. Stand back and let us guide you, then look back again and see what's changed. In your own speed and time let it all unfold. To learn and grow will need a lot of acceptance and focusing. Search until you find the missing parts and then look where they fit in. You are being told and given signals. Stop if not sure and wait for further teachings. Let the sun and the moon lighten up your path. The timing is of essence and you would be wise to listen. Throughout the night you get the deepest answers and healing back to be able to do what you are here for. Relax in between so you can focus on your work. Tonight will be a time when clues are given to many. The time to empty out and understand what's been said is beneficial.

Joy and health from the whole team. TttA

TRANSFORMATION!

It's a privilege to be able to see a transformation and at times transfiguration. You have seen that many times. It's a part of your study. So keep it all as a test and skill. Many others will come to you and ask, and then you know what to say. Your part is often to pass on information that in time will make the transformation. The transfiguration is also a tool to be able to see another life time or get an answer to a question. You have often seen that working if and when something needs to heal or get an explanation.

There is just one way. We have many other ways, but you are all so differently made up, so tools to suit today's event are coming up and you will be able to deal with it. All is well and will stay well and improve as the time passes. Stay cheerful and relax to help you to meet situations in the best possible way. Go on with your other workload to advance and help.

Love and light to all. From TttA

EARLY START!

Good morning, glad tidings once again. The sun is coming closer to you so enjoy the warmth and growth that the sun will give you. After a long time on your path you are seeing the light a lot faster. It could not have happened before all other conditions have come in to order. The time is still important, so stay as you are for a little longer. We are working to help and encourage you, so you can get the inspiration for your work. More interests are also installed for you about your workbooks paintings and the group, because of the changes in the universe, you are altering the timeslots. That is to be flexible and welcome the growth. Today will tell a story, so wait and see. Carry out what's on your plate today, it will be to your benefit and leave tomorrow to us. Enjoy today and let the time go as it may. The future is not yet clear, but you can smell it. Now, security and safety is for us to deal with.

Blessings for you and all that support you. TttA

ALL IN GOOD TIME!

If and when things don't eventuate, the timing is out. You know that is so because of other situations that are not sorted. Cooperation even more so in the spirit world, afterwards you can look back and see why and how things happened. Express your thoughts, feelings and actions, and then you will see how well planned all is and always will be. Once again we are always reminding you about so many old truths, that you at times have forgotten. Enjoy and recharge in the sun and fresh air. You know very well that's beneficial for you. Whoever comes to you in your place is sent by us, so welcome them and treat them as we want you to do. Keep on adding colours and spice in to your life. It will give you strength and vigour. Still alter a few things and you will notice a change in the atmosphere. It will refresh all that comes, that's OK too. Study life and you will have a better knowledge about human nature.

Eternal blessings to you all. TttA

UNFOLDING TIME!

A natural unfolding is recommended now. Still do your part as we have said. Leave all situations to be sorted by us. You are learning to surrender and that's good, keep it up. As you do that your trust in us and a few people will also increase. Life is not always plain sailing. Storm breezes and gusts are a part of the forces that are moving and make you aware of water and energies. Study the different effects that come with it. So wind rain and storm, because of the energies and clearing cleansing of many things. Others withdraw into security and safety. The makeup of a person is normally what early experiences or feelings from a long time ago have happened. Most times the physical gets affected. Sensitive people and animals feel the forces stronger. There are also many that react differently at different times, and there are many shades and levels of development. It's all a learning curve and to be able to see and study yourself and others. As the earth is now moving further in the photon belt it will alter your distance to the planets and their effects.

Keep on opening your eyes and listen in. TttA

ASK FOR A POSITIVE SOLUTION!

Yes my children ask and you will receive. We do have your best interest at heart. Remember also to ask for divine timing, you might think that you are ready and you are many times, but others will need more time to prepare and get ready. So wait, don't be impatient only follow through our guide lines and all will turn out for the highest good. Look again in to the core why and how it happened and what did you learn from it. If you don't see why, you will get the same lesson again and again, until you learn and advance. Later on you will get deeper truth and lessons. So you will advance higher up your climb to the top of your goal. Also keep in mind that these are individual lessons and only walk on your path. Don't ever do a copycat journey. That would not help you or others. People would not learn anything from it and all need to understand that spiritual growth comes from the source and your willingness to accept the truth. Always give thanks for help, healing and holiness. We are rejoicing every time you are open to give love and light to yourself and others.

Strength and love from us all. TttA

COMMUNICATION!

Be careful about what's going on and who is picking up the wrong end of the communication. Make sure that you have a clear line, before you get any more information. Some people can't or won't hear you or are blaming hearing or selective hearing and worst don't understand and never ask again. So they will go away thinking along distorted lines. Tonight will bring a clearer and better understanding for all concerned. At the moment the universe is altering of planets and energies so a little mix up is still apparent now and then. All you can do is to be an observer and ask for the words and thoughts to be sent out. Ask for more specific help and listen in. Some people have been so wounded so they like to think they know it all and let everyone know it. It's only a way of wanting to be heard. Respect others and let us explain a deeper understanding of what's going on. Learn more as you go along what's on your plate. The interference is great but it's only temporary.

Courage and wisdom. TttA

STUDY THE MOTIVE, WHY HAVE THEY COME!

Be an anchor and ask what and why you have connected. Let us tell you we know you now, so this is a reminder again. We have spoken to other spirits and called them to act now. Many hear my voice and cut out the message others activate their spirit connection and search for more. Knowledge is fine but again we say wisdom is better. When where and how you should act for the best result. So many times human souls are so complex and puzzled so wait if not sure. That's why we so often say the situation is right but not the timing as yet. Unfolding time is proven to be time consuming because of the tangled webs many weave.

Long-time tangling will take long time to untangle and understand. Life is often full of signs and why and how the thread goes and where it comes from. Enigmas of life are there for you all to make good use of them all and to learn if and when it will happen. Stop and stand back, after you will see what the lesson has been. Open up to a wider scope of wisdom.

Love and wisdom. TttA

STAND BY!

When and how, ask us and remember to empty out first other ways how can you receive more. Too many forget which is understandable but not advisable. This time when all the universal forces are at work, take one day at the time. You all think that is a lot and to repeat it so often, but very sound advice indeed. We are relying on every one of you to do so. Put in to action what you have been trained for, we know that you can, so do it. Mighty other forces are doing their best to influence life on your planet, but it only causing little ripples on the water, down to the bottom of the sea or being sent back to the source with love and light. Many monkeys have come to you now for a while, hoping that you will send them love and light to go back to the source. That's working fine but keep in mind to detach and empty out after. No one can be able to receive when your system is full of all other subjects and dates. Go ahead today and carry out our input. May our light be a blessing upon your path.

Blessings and love. TttA

LOOK BEHIND THE SCENES!

To discover what lies behind the actions or the unexplained events it's usually the best help you can get. Always look deeper than most do. The amount of masks that many people carry with them is at times very deceptive. Look again in to the eyes of the person and listen to what's been said. Also take notice of what you feel in their company. If unease is present, stop and ask for the person to be checked and cleaned up from other visitors. Many carry others pain worries and distortions for years without knowing it. You have seen many examples of that. Teach others how to recognise the interference. Always stand back and detach otherwise you cannot see the tangled webs. Ask for a better way to make sure that all is well. The time before next jolt of earth is crucial. Stay firm compassionate and loving. Many react to your knowledge but they don't know it's really ours. You will notice many reactions at times because they know, because they neither know nor have not recognised the truth yesterday revealing time was very important. You did sense that something was wrong. That is a start.

Carry on and expose more of it with love and light. TttA

LET THE COLOUR OF THE RAINBOW INFILTRATE YOU!

Yes that is a very good thing to have all the different healing vibrations gives you a good start of the day. A good start is very important for your energy that's needed for you the whole day. Remember times past when no colour was present how grey everything was. Use colours in healing including gems to enhance your homes health and harmony. Look at your environment how do the colours affect you? Learn about how to alter colours to help you feel better when to tense or similar use. Soft shades other times be flexible and see what you can do to make your journey easier and more and more joyful. Beware still of sales man that want to get rid of something,also mind hypnosis. There are many ways to trap a soul, but look at the signs and you will stay clear of rocks and old ship wrecks. Well now you are having a good start once again. Blessing for today and all you meet along your travels.

Joy, calm and health! TttA

HOLD ON AND DO CHEER UP!

We know how much work is being done in the name of the light through you and it will be done for a long time. As you grow your energy will also increase many will notice and many will not like it because of their own little scams will be exposed and then all other situations that are connected will be revealed also. It's all got to do with the big sort out before the photon belts connection. The Earth has already entered the belt, but some don't think so, let them be, don't ever try to convince anyone about the truth. It will not help their spirit to get told when not a question has been heard or told. Let them come when they are ready we will plant the seed and then your part comes in to it. You have been trained so keep on doing your part unfold in its natural course. We are still waiting for other souls that are not quite ready, all are developing at different speeds. So leave all that to us. You are still a builder not the architect. Divine order is the best way.

Strength and wisdom for all. TttA

THE CHRIST IN ME SALUTE THE CHRIST IN YOU!

That is a very important statement. All living things have a chance to salute the living Christ that comes and lives in everyone that are open to the light and love from the source. Remember to invite the healing light so that you all can function and be like the Christ spirit to evolve is to learn and listen in. You all have a natural independent way but that's not enough. To take advice is not always easy but if you want to advance look for guidelines. It's always there but sometimes hidden because the soul is not yet ready so the knowledge could be misused. The right tools in the wrong hands smell danger. The same pattern goes for gem stones. Many could easily to use them in a negative way's a lesson that you all should take notice of the first thing when you want to know anything be an observer and then study the pattern and see the picture. To know all the facts is advisable, if you don't wrong decisions will be made. And time and energy wasted.

See you again tonight TttA

KEEP IN CLOSE CONTACT!

Let our love and light draw you closer to us and refresh and restore you. Last night was another test for many of you all. As we said and will say again, when warning bells are ringing listen. It's too easy when tired to get slack on all the protections. Don't ever take for granted that all is automatic and you don't have to do your work. Learn how to cooperate and let the bells ring before entering in to anything. Too many do not believe or take notice of warnings. They are infant fools as it does not cost anything to listen, but also it will cost you in energy depletion if you don't. The work balance was given to you all this morning. That is a way to not over do or under do. To grow you all need a balance in your life, if one area is not activated the others will get out of balance. All doing their own part in there long chain of events and life styles. Keep going in your speed today.

Blessings and wisdom. TttA

FRESHNESS AND JOY FROM THE SPIRIT!

Enjoy the new start for today. You all need to have just that. Thinking too much or too little is not making you have a balance. We all have been watching you and your progress, so keep on doing as you are. When time is out ask why and we will tell you. It's normally a lesson to be learned. Or a situation that's need to be clarified. Recently you have been given practical examples of many parts of your teachings from us. So many different levels of understanding and so much of growth for some. It's all in the stages of climbing up and rest when we advise. Take time to ponder and accept the universal truth. It's a long journey for most searching souls also to keep in mind further dealings with others that are individual as we have said many times before, treat everyone as an individual soul never two alike similar but not exactly the same. That does not mean that you have to spend more time with one after talking with us, you will know how and when. You are the middle person so learn how to accept your part.

Love and cheers from TttA

ORDER!

Tangled situations are not for any that's working for the light. You are being trained so do your untangling and aid to get a straight line to order and light. The same goes for all disorganized souls, and pathways. We will give you real signs and you will easily put them up when you are moving around in many areas. We will guide you how and where will be best. Then it's up to the person taking notice or not. Never order anyone, we suggest and teach so will you. Always pass on our teaching when we advise to do so. Most people do not want to be told. So that will also hinder their ways of thinking and their free will. Learn and study more about the human nature, it's quite complex and has unresolved situations hidden very deep and instead of burying it let it come out to the surface to look at and be released to the universe, the source of all good. Enjoy todays work and go ahead one more step upwards. Glory to the creator and Father.

Blessings from TttA

BETTER AND BETTER EVERY DAY!

Let that truth go in to your very soul. You know, so training times are here. Stay firm about your discipline. Let go of thoughts that are trying to disrupt you, especially at the weekends. You do know and how they operate. One day it will stop and, you will free to live as you were meant to. The warmth is coming back. Enjoy the newness and welcome all that's good and joyful. We have seen your trials and tribulations. Yes we have seen that so many have being trying to disrupt or injure you, and also many that have your best interests at heart. Give it time and the sort out will be done. Too many situations that are very complex stop and detach after finishing a job. All the maintenance was important. Keep your spirit work in the same order. The colours are coming back in your garden so look, enjoy and be thankful for all little pictures you are being shown. Leave your life to us to sort out.

Smile again and say thanks. TttA

EXCHANGE IS VERY GOOD!

Let my spirit be with you the whole day and you will benefit by it all in all areas. Back to surrendering you still don't know it all so one day at a time. Once more let the rain today bring you freshness and light, to clear up or wash away, it will help you to see what's going on. We know but you at times can't see for one reason or the other. The opposition's favourable tools are to confuse people and let them stay there. If and when you feel like that that is the situation, ask for it to be lifted so you can get on with your work. Don't try to save the day when it's not up to you. So many others are involved and they have to learn to make their own decisions. Waiting could become a trap also when you become tempted to act out of boredom. Watch out and do something different. Practical solutions are a good way to deal with it. Today will also tell a story which way and when will you learn? We are standing by. The pattern of your life has started to emerge when the book file turned up at last.

Cheers and love from us all. TttA

STAY CALM IN THE STORM!

Don't get ruffled feathers if and when if and when you come across diversity and anger. Unresolved feelings and emotions and inflow of any kind is coming to the surface and stirring more emotions. If you feel that coming up look at it professionally and see why it's best not to bury anything. Let it out, not necessary in anger but in emotional intelligence. Don't get over or under expressible. You will have to balance all feelings as much as possible so you both can get a chance to listen and talk. Saying what you want and feel is essential. To come across as plainly as possible is the best. Keep on learning and listen to us and your fellow man. Keep on going as your progress is coming up again and waiting time is over. Slowly does it you can't see as yet only feel the changes? The light is shining on your path so keep going straight ahead. We are still with you and support healing and joy in full measure is there to aid you on your journey. Many tasks and events to enlighten you and re-join the link with it all. Thank you.

Blessings and light from us all. TttA

ONE MORE TASK FINISHED!

Stay clear of people that are trying to disturb you. Focus all your energy on yourself and positive students. Your system is getting stronger. So stay calm and strong so you can get to the perfect condition. We strongly reinforce and let others also know how you can handle situations similar to that. The sound of the music will also aid you in your balance quest. Let my love and light enhance your decisions. It's all a test for you forever learning and understanding. Life as you have seen it is an everlasting school class. With exams and teachers with a head master. The parables are always useful so you can understand and remember our teachings. Some might think as you as a student of light don't need to study/.wrong again. The higher you go the more time apart with us to faster get your part to activate in the big chain of life. Let it all unfold naturally. We do know where you are at all times. So think about us and we are there.

Love and congratulations. TttA

SEARCH FOR ETERNAL JOY!

Don't let the glitter and glamour fool you in to thinking that is what you have been looking for. The internal search and quest for life's answers are to look inside your soul and get a glint of heavenly beauty. The psychical is only an overcoat that the divine spirit lives in. Many have called the body the temple but really the spirit is the temple that connects you to the source and us. Keep all in order by discipline and focus. We can't say that often enough. It's the spiritual and universal law in operation. You will go were your work takes you. In your case you do your travel at night with us, because you will be given instructions of next day's work and also receive healing for yourself. Past traumas needed extra attention so love and learn. At the moment events and people are stitched up being forced to look at their situations that is not was most people want, now is a good time. Please remember to leave the work to us at the end of the day. More tomorrow.

Testing times once again. TttA

KNOWLEDGE IS NOT ENOUGH!

To have the know-how is fine, but how to know how to apply it in wisdom is another thing. You have been working on that now for years, and still it's a quarry at times but now you can understand others better. You can't take sides but stand in the middle and see both sides. That's a good mediator and also activator. Be completely detached and unemotional to be able to deal with the situation. It's always a reason why someone acts as they do. Back to the seven deadly sins when you can see where it's coming from. Actions always lead to reactions but don't forget rejections. It's energy and can be misused or used for a good solution. The same goes for gems they are tools, but in the wrong hands they could cause a lot of harm and the opposite to performing miracles. We will inform you how to best use your tools. We have entrusted you with many so use them wisely. Protect and keep clean from spirit pollution. My sun and the salty living waters will keep them in good working order. Let the warmer weather invigorate you and all you are connected with.

Cheers and strength be with you. TttA

THE LIGHT AND LOVE NETWORK!

Let no one disturb or destroy the network of most importance. That's there to hold a safety net over the earth and its inhabitants. Visualise all that and encourage others to do the same. Let the planet be surrounded by everlasting arms with love and light from the universal store house. Feel the warmth and strength coming in to you and aid your life to grow in all areas that are needed. Keep the flames burning and fill up the fuel so the flame will never stop giving out. Keep in mind what we have told you and store some in your spirit bank for further use and to care. Today it will be another change to restore your life. The now computing situations will get sorted and you will get an explanation. Or get better. You live mostly in another dimension so it will need a deep understanding from you to get your message across. Keep on delivering our wisdom and love and all will be well.

Deepest love and thanks' from TttA

CARRY OUT TODAYS WORK!

Go on your path to sort and sift what's going to aid you on your journey. Many times you have asked why so many incidents and tests on your path! That's why you were sent to New Zealand to clear up old work situations and go back to where you come from rather NZ is a part of an old out post to the old Lemur ian (Mu) for short. The knowledge from that time will still be used many times. You will and you shall that's a promise. Some days nothing is happening that because other areas are being activated and made ready for the whole solution. The team work is very important but because of different abilities for different people needs to be updated and dusted off. In the meantime you have to wait and let all concerned be joined into a long chain and a battle for the force. Bless every day as you will have another chance to work and love. Unwind with what we give you of ideas people and meetings. The ones that help you will be blessed for ever.

Amen and truth. TttA

BLESSED ARE THE MEEK AND LOWLY!

Don't ever underestimate the meek and lowly. All have their own place in life and when the society rejects some for not fitting in and you don't accept them, they are not very developed or loving. Society today is made for the 3rd dimension and you and many others are not there anymore, so you are able to see the difference. When I said let there be light, I meant it. Light in all souls and growing love in their hearts. That would evolve your world and it would be much easier to accept the universal teachings and truth. Also to remember to empty out and very calmly take in what we are giving you. When no information is given wait for new input and do what you have to do for all mankind. That is a part of making up for lost opportunities and help to aid many kinds of evolvements further in to the photon belt.

Blessings and wisdom from all your teachers' helpers and students. TttA

BLESSINGS!

Let's enjoy today and give out plenty of blessings to all. Yesterday's work was extra good. You did follow through what was your part of the chain of events. The way things operate in the universe is not commonly known to many. Spread the word about. First surrender to the source and then wait for input. When it comes check and make sure that you have the light station on the line. You in your case will feel when it's right or wrong. Others might want to learn. The fresh wind today is clearing the air and letting you know what's going on. Your own change of energy is very vital for your work and your growth. Go ahead with your alterations and you will see more quickly what's happening. Tonight is a point of interest as to how some will react when studying them you will know without saying anything where they are. Not to judge only to see how they operate and on what level. Only to practise how to recognise actions and reactions. Read, relax and rejoice for the rest of the day. The force is with you and your work.

Love light and joy. TttA

START FRESH ONCE MORE!

When one door shuts another will open. Meaning one chapter has been worked on ended so another can start will not happen if you don't have understood. The lesson in it all. Look at it as a school exam then you can easily see way see why some situations take longer than others to resolve. We your team are always the same never changing never forsaking always supporting you. Trial times are here again, you now have to stand back from it and leave it for us to deal with. You cannot be expected to do our work, one day you will and then you can help others like we are doing now. You have asked to see us, its coming but it has taken a little longer than first thought. Things are altering and it makes it hard to say exactly when. Patience is still a big part of your training. And now you have seen how much you still have to learn. Keep going as we suggest and please do your best to unwind in between. Forever working without stopping is not advisable. Enjoy today change and do your work with us.

Eternal blessings. TttA

TAKE STOCK!

Today is a time to look at who is who and make believe, too many are pretending to be white and they are in reality quite black. The genuine keeps going and don't let other people down, and the other keeps all things before they get exposed for what they are. Keep on looking at their eyes and you soon will be able to tell where they are. Pray for a stronger protection and shield and surrender to the source every morning. The fresh air and the practical work will bring you back to reality. As much as we do now about people's motives, still it does not happen as intended. Interference from other sources that wanting a big piece of the cake (energy). My child of light you have once again been in a battle for the good of all mankind. The sadness from the onslaught was great this time. Give yourself same time out. And be outside. The little child that come to us yesterday was grateful for all help received, it would have been worse if she have carried on living on earth. Keep on sending prayers for her and her family. Thank you.

Forever yours and clarity will be given. TttA

LET GO AND LET GOD THE FATHER AND CREATOR IN!

Too many people all tangled up will at this point cause disturbance and anger because of old hurts and old anger can't stay down any longer. It comes up to the surface and is exposed. The truth hurts and most do not want to see or hear what has to be dealt with. If not dealt with they cannot be in the photon belt area. If only all would sort out their situations. We are very willing to aid all. Life after life more and more lessons should be learned. At times you know but it's not so easy to know where to start. That's why we often remind you about one step at a time will do it. Rest and follow today's energy, too many different situations on the horizon. Be outside when you feel that you need solitude and peace. The new Christ conciseness time is getting closer so prepare yourself and ask for help when not a clear guidance is given. Time is manmade so let it all unfold in its own space and eternal timing.

Care and blessings for all today. TttA

ORDER!

Order in all things will benefit all and all you deal with. Let no one stop you when you are working for spirit you are in a position to have all aid and protection going at all times. Let today be a day of reunion refreshment and re-connecting. Tell others that it really is simple if you follow through our teachings and don't stray from your path. The temptations are many at present time and If and when we are trying our best to reach you, obstacles come in the way. Today will also bring a little more harmony and joy between souls. That's good. You all have so many different talents so use them together to make a strong deterrent for all negative inputs. Stay flexible and joyful for the work to be done faster. Go ahead today and make the most of it. It will turn out fine, as so many want to be taken notice of or loved one way or the other so they often lash out or change time or ideas fast. Let them come and give them to us for help in all areas.

Love and light and wisdom. TttA

LATE AGAIN!

Yes we know. How many times that happened, but it was for a good reason. You get some practical help and when other people's situations are involved you need to be flexible and understanding. If and when you are a little delayed it's for a reason also. To walk in someone else shoes is to see a life of another human not before you know. Then you can see more clearly. Many have come to you with tangled situations, but that was good you have plenty of experience and with our help you help them to see what's going on. It does not help if you don't look into the core with patience and focus. Expose what has been covered and fill in the missing pieces so you can see the framework and which colour fits wherever know that your work is to bearing fruit that has been a very long time coming but you have been faithful for years now so much to look at and sort out from so many lifetimes ago. Your training has been quite severe but it was necessary for all involved.

Blessings and love from. TttA

BLESSED BE AND STAY!

Think about that truth and what I have said before. Only for 24 hours each time. I have promised blessings and help of all kinds. We just said that so many life time's ago. At times it will take more than that to understand the universal spirit eons. It would be too much to take in when the knowledge input is not accepted. Be aware of those who tell you otherwise always temptations and to easily to give up and let go of development. Rest a while when tired and relax in the nature- water and air will refresh you. Mostly water. Many are so in need and want of new energy so to try anything at times would be a side track. Understandable but not advisable. Go ahead with your life and always trust even if you wonder why and how the solution will come. Back to the prayers give us today our daily bread that means all of your wants but only what's best for your higher self. Also the saying God might not come when I want- but he is usually right on time.

Blessings for tonight. TttA

CLEAR THINKING AND ACTIONS!

Give the communication a thought, is it getting through or not. At times you know straight away, other times it will come during sleep. Whenever you are ready the solution is given. Let us do the organisation and give you what's needed for your higher self. To clear and clean out once again lighten up your aura. Let the light and love flow from your place and they will return. You have promised to let us use, your home as a station and healing place and we are doing just that. Go on your path today and let it all unfold naturally. Last night was very connected with an old contact from another life time from so long time ago. The little brave Cheyenne girl will succeed and go very far. Support will be given and she will return to you as she did so long time ago. She knew it was a sign of her spirit opening up. The join up time is here and much old soul will return to you and your sanctuary for different kinds of help and solutions. It's all planned by us. And you will help to activate part of it, what is on your path way.

Blessings in full measure from your loving teachers. TttA

STARS AND LIGHT!

Let us guide and enlighten you all the way to your goal. Don't let anything daunts your spirit. Many have tired,many different ways to tempt mislead or belittle you. It did not work. Some will give up and some trying something else. Why you wonder? They are only looking for energy to live on because they are lazy not to do their own homework like you have done for so many years now. Very few understand what that is all about. That's not your concern so leave it to us. As we keep on saying. Repetition is the core of all knowledge, and as we today are helping you to celebrate we wish for you to feel our nearness and love. Keep going as you are we know how hard you are trying and starting up again and again. The will power to succeed is eternally yours as a gift from us. Keep on asking for assistance an in an instant we are with you. Let us unveil a little at a time. Help and wisdom is given freely also.

Love and light. TttA

BLESSINGS TO ALL LIVING THINGS!

Blessed be and stay that way. Too many people are confused bewildered and talked in to things. Beware of the ones that push or prod in to your life without being asked. Help given might have been well meant but acts as a put down or belittlement for others. We say leave well alone. It's a neglect from that that gets so many in the strife. Don't think for a moment that is the first action to be followed without checking out. The negative are expert to bring other people down or pretend to be something they never will be nor have an idea about. The same as the old parable the first shall be the last. It's a big turnover at present. All the ones high up in the church think they don't have to do any work on themselves. Wrong, the higher you go the more work in the withdrawal and meditation is necessary. No one is to say or do anything before asking advice and wisdom from us. To be seen to act without knowing the whole picture is to be a fool. Still I say send love and light to all. The once that help you will be blessed for ever. Then back to the source for us to deal with.

Think upon this truth TttA

ASK FOR CLARIFICATION!

When you don't see what's going ask for a clear picture with guidance. Be an onlooker and stand back to be able to see better. Last week was a good indication about actions and people. Most of them see you their way, they perceiving you in their understanding few have started to see who you are and they have open their eyes to peoples level of wisdom and acceptance. Remember that is not what you always think some can't tell you the truth of fear of being rejected or not welcome. Past trauma and events will play a part of all that. Speak your mind wait and see. Unfolding time is not so easy many scary for some a relief for others that's why the communication gets hard between souls, let us do the connection first. Preparations are very important because you want to have a good outcome. The picture how to care for your garden will help you also to remember as long as you have seasons used them wisely. The whole universe is still changing. Make the most of each blessed day and keep on loving aiding and lighten some burden. Tell them about the surrendering each morning.

Thank you for your part. TttA

FACT OR FICTION!

Let's talk about what's going on. You all are waiting for news but that's not surprising. The whole universe is in uproar and so much is changing. Stay calm and steady we are doing all we can to help, your situations. It's all different but you know that already. Circumstances are not always clear but it will be dealt with. The high temperature is also disturbed so many. Today's quake was also expected to happen. It will be more before it all have settle down. Pace yourself and don't act before you get the OK. You have asked for more facts. Fiction seems to be rising up on the horizon at present. Too many have the so called truth to tell others add on to the picture don't listen too much. Some have a part of it and added and others interpret the message the way the spirit comes in. but whose spirit and whose truth. Stay very clear and detach for now. Patience is called for and love and laughter at least try your best and we will do the rest. Joy in the blessings you do have. Beware of falsehood and so called facts. Stand back and relax for now.

Blessings and strength. TttA

LOVE AND LIGHT TO ALL!

Let your love and light go to all that need it. Don't ask how just do as we ask you. Too many are in strife and pain at the present, because of conditions not being dealt with from so long time ago. To bury something or someone is not always the best solution. Exposure is not the easiest either. Pain anger and unforgivness and hate are often better dealt with instead of regress down and bury it all. If you don't understand what to do ask us and then get the answer how and what to do. To get a clear picture of what really did happen not what someone told you in their opinion and fashion. Second hand hearsay is not a good way to act upon. Get it straight away from the source. Still do have compassion and listen in to what's needed to solve the maze of tangle events. Have a spell out when you can't see don't stay to close applies also. To be an observer is very good. Stand by and don't let anything disturb your home and sanctuary. That's the way you will help others, by opening up your home to so many searching souls.

Blessing to you and the entire one that's helping you. TttA

WATCH OUT FOR TRANSFERAL!

Yes my children watch out for what is transferred to you from spirit, mind emotion and body. So often you don't notice when it happens. You would do well to be more vigilant. Watch for changes in actions and thoughts and language. Be a good observer and listen in. Too many people don't give another person a chance to express themselves or they will be sending out expressions and feelings and vibrations that's an expression of frustration or anger. Keep the balance and try to walk in each other's shoes for a short time. We know that you are doing just that but so many times after being abused and used you lose hope and wonder why. When the message doesn't get through leave it to us. We know it all and can give you all. Waiting is not easy, keep steady and so happy as possible and we will do the rest. All last night's communication was all about the past life's conditions. So long ago and so much tribal war fare. Use the wisdom and spread love to be able to bridge so many waters. To be a mediator is not anyone's path is another lesson for you to eternity. To learn is to grow.

Blessings. TttA

ONWARDS AND UPWARDS!

Remember that is the one key to growth. Concentrate and learn. Focus and relax and all priorities will fall in to the right order. Go on your way today to test the waters you will find out a little more each time. Try and try again might sound very demanding but that is another way you can learn. The only time you let go is to get a better grip. Its O K to change your mind when unease is in the air. Understand that we are standing in your corner and we are supporting you in your quest. Try to unwind a little more and play music when you connect with us. Music has a very beneficial input for your very spirit. Big task has been dealt with in the last few months. Not completed yet but well on its way. As the weather stabilises so will you. Your system is responding to change too much, so stay calm and keep on building your fort for a safe haven for yourself and the one that has been sent to you. You never will get easy situations to deal with and practise on so accept your work with a smile.

Loving thoughts from us all. TttA

WITHDRAW TO GET A CLEAR VIEW!

So many are in the mist and in between lands. Most find it very hard to know when or what to do so they are ending up absolutely doing nothing. It's alright when we say so but also remember that it's a different path for everyone. And you can't give them any personal service if you give out personal advice for the masses. Personal growth is only directed for that person. General advice country or state will benefit in a collective situation. The same applies for karmic conditions, man or country karma will be dealt with so when some wondering why not all got killed in a disaster they were not in that karmic pocket. Other time is the other way around. Present time is cleaning up and clearing time. Old wounds needed to heal by expressions of love and light and after start afresh. Quite often you and many others have been told believable truth but it turned out to be a side tracked version once again. Surrender once again every morning and night and leave it to us.

Enjoy the sun and fresh air as much as possible when you can.

Trust and acceptance from us all. TttA

FRESH WIND IN YOUR SAILS!

Today we are close to you in your thoughts. The sorting out time is still here. You are wondering often how long and what year will it all get done. Well that's an on-going task only periods of time sometimes less. It's according to work. How much has been accumulating around you. Also before next level you need to be clean and clear so that you can be refilled with more truth and more wisdom. You and many others will be touch by our love and light so all you have to do is pass it on. We know how you feel at times when too many are ready and don't want to learn more for your own learning you must be patient and wait. Remember long ago when you did ask about timing we gave you a watch in good order that's why you don't have to ask anymore. Just wait and you will see and hear. Yesterday's news will be dealt with in its own good time. And you will hear the full story. You wonder many times you seems to be the last one anyone tells. Your intuition is very strong so you just know when things are not right.

Blessings for today. TttA

TEMPTATIONS AND SHADOWS!

Thus two things could easily cause many broken hearts and many angry reactions. Watch out for that and see why it's happening, and what we learn from it. Nothing is for nothing so learn from your connections. Don't make a statement before you stand back and see what's going on and after clearing away thoughts that are no longer wanted. You have so many times for more ways and more positive input. In your case it has to be gradual, because of your system. Nothing is wrong only different to show you another angle of life. Your personal situation will be sorted. You have been told why and what your job was, so leave it all for now. Don't despair or be despondent many would love to see you out of the picture. Why do they still waste their .time? Past life time's connections are surfacing again. Look and learn once again. Start afresh and enjoy life. Once in a while you have been used and abused so the scars are deep and many. Value where you are and try to see why your mind will be clear and just be.

Blessings and healing. TttA

WATCH OUT FOR CONTROLLING OPINIONS!

At times you have seen so many situations that need clarification. You know when you don't get through and others are very willing to play games. Don't by in to that thought pattern that has nothing to do with your work. Others will see and try to stop what they think they can. Instead they would be advised to look in to their own back yard. It's so easy for some to find fault in others that's only a reflection of themselves. Stay clear of that kind of thoughts that will only take you away from your real work. Everyone has his or her own path way and progress to work on. All others need to look in to their own silence and their own lessons in life. Go ahead today and enjoy the little changes and alterations in energy. Last night showed up for what it really was and how energy can alter. Watch and wait in the meantime. You will see and hear more soon. Stay steady and it has nothing to do with you. Only attacks against the light.

Blessings and light. TttA

DON'T LOOK BACK!

Yes that was obvious what someone was saying. No one can keep going if not authentic Make believers and on hangers are of no use to you or not even to themselves. Of late you have shown who is who and what they are working on plus look for their motives. You did ask so you got the picture. Sad story but we will deal with it as for now you have given it back to us. Look at it as a learning curve. It was very clear where they are and that will help you in the future to see and understand why people act as they do. Desperations give them ideas and clues, at times boredom and hunger for a change. Watch and listen a little more and they will be exposed for what they are. If not genuine it will come out sooner or later and even later on today you will hear more news. Most people do not realize who you are and who you are working for. All you have to do is carry on working as usual but cut off the connection when the drainage is too much and once more we are with you and the ones that hurt you will be dealt with by us.

Blessings and joy. TttA

REST AND SURRENDER!

So many times you have done just that. It shows you how wonderful it is. Divine timing and intervention is how the source operates. Today once again you met 3 unwanted souls. That is a part of the pattern. You will experience more miracles soon. The opposition knows how close you are to the next advancement so they are doing their very best to put you off. You did have other tasks done that did confirm that all is in working order. You know that is so enjoying what you can and trust that we are renewing part of you that was needed. You did ask so we heard your prayers. Your faith and trust is also being challenged. The supplies that you need are being delivered so trust and surrender every day. Nothing is impossible for us. People will start to listen to you rather to us more so empty out and be prepared. Rest and smile whenever you can, it will help to unwind and you will more easily understand what's going on. Mysteries are not always easy to solve, so leave it to us.

Blessings and joy from us all. TttA

ENJOY AND RESTORE!

Let today be a day of restoration before the new Christ energy descending to Earth next month. There will be a big clean up and many disturbances. All for a good cause. It's hurting for a little while but the big improvement is going to help all and aid all mankind. All the planetary changes on you planet are upsetting to so many, especially sensitive people. Only for a short time now and you can take a little breather. It's quite tiring so be on your guard. The only thing you really have to do is surrender to us. Many of you don't want to ask for help but how else you can get the activation. We said you are daughter and sons of a king and at times sitting in rags. Ask and claim big things and it will come. Cooperation with spirit is essential value for all. Yesterday's sort out was not nice but it needed to be done. The will of the father is the will of creation and stop and think what the meaning of today's events is. Let the sun enliven and restore you for coming times when you all will be doing your part of the light workers cooperation with the source.

Eternal blessings. TttA

LET THE DAY UNFOLD!

Let us deal with the unfolding and also let us be in charge of your blue print. You don't always see it but when you surrender day and night you still have to make the final decision and after trying and practising for a while you get to know what's best for you and your higher self. The only things that are really counting are the growth of spirit and that's way you have been getting so many tests lately. It was only for you to test your abilities about spiritual and universal law. Back to the main core of understanding and wisdom. Some days you feel like to withdraw for the whole day. That's O K in your case, because you need to digest what's what and take stock. We have been watching you close and from afar for a long time. Your understandings are getting clearer and take shorter time to get through. Tonight we will come again and protect advice and support you and your work. Trust only in the life force and don't get caught up in the net of mass media that is spinning at the moment.

Encourage and accept us all. TttA

WATER YOUR SPIRIT GARDEN!

Let' do some watering to day. You experience a lot of feeling yesterday. Some hot, some cold but that is normal for now. Stand back and say your piece and we will do the rest. Before you do anything sit back and relax for you to be able to receive any knowledge and valuable information. Many places and many races are entangled and try to make their own way according to their belief. Really it's only a different aspect of the same thing. Small minded people and narrow minded thinkers have to go to make room for new ideas and a better way to look at life and spiritual growth. People's eyes come in to it and then it will be tangled. Ask and plan big things and ask us to take care of it in a special way. All personal events are coming to the surface and are being dealt with. Let all emotions be outside the discussion. Clear facts and the truth will come out. Too many make believers and ego trips. Be patient and stand by for more input. It's still sort out time.

Eternally yours. TttA

CARRY ON AS YOU HAVE STARTED!

Go on as we say a little at a time. It does not matter how much time it takes it's only the end result that counts. The goal so many at this time are trying to solve all at once. That is not a good way. You all have your ideas and solutions some think they know it all and they are trying to convince others. That how it is. The ego and wanting to be right is the small percentage and then they are filling in the rest themselves. Let us do the work and whatever we think you are able to do we let you know. Many do not like to have a master but a positive one will enable you to have free will. The interference is great at present but it is a waste of time. Stay clear steady and calm. The sun and the water will aid you. When no input for action is given do your duties and wait. People and situation are very much in an altered state of mind. The negative will get worse and the positive will advance and go forth. No one should be judged before the last day of their living.

Grace and love to all. TttA

RESTORE AND REVALUATE!

That's a very valuable way to get a clear prospect of your life. Today so far it has been a lot of that going on in the hidden places. Treasures were found and other situations got sorted. Now you can have a fresh view of everything. The same goes for your spirit life, when you want a fresh outlook of where you are and to be able to understand others that come to you. Like the time so long ago when the old vine looked dead and needed pruning to give new shoots a chance to grow. All that lovely energy must come out. That is the law of nature. That's also why the old parables needed to be understood and used. All situations not understood is a waste, so think of them as a practical story that will benefit you and others. Too much of and too much advanced thinking will fall on stony ground if not explained in terms of knowledge in the amiable language when you ask what level to use, and then the soul will learn and connect.

Eternal teaching and wisdom from TttA

LET US COMMUNICATE!

That is really the most important part of the day. Check and empty out so you are able to receive knowledge and help in all forms. Keep in mind to read the "input level" you must first know where the person is and what level.

That was what we talked about yesterday but quite a few just talks and send out messages and hope for the best. The wisdom will only get through to some souls the rest will fall on stony ground. Use language for the biggest part when in a crowd otherwise sit calm and ask us which approach to use. Where you now live is a big mixture of back grounds and beliefs. So establish first where to start. Let the experience of yesteryears guide you and build on that. The groundwork and base is the most valuable way to start, as well as the foundation in a building. Let today be an "open up day" and unite and learn the strength of a team at the same time. When apart draw on the energy from the connection of the groups. Time apart is essential for growth, and more time to reflect.

Wisdom from TttA

ONWARDS AND UPWARDS!

My children of light that is a good solid start of the day. Go ahead and recharge in your garden of delight. The greens and all the nature energy is of all benefit for you. The fresh air and the sounds of your birds will all help to invigorate you for coming times and is an eventful time as in a way you are all waiting for the Christ energy to descend to earth and give you what you require. The guardians and keepers also will let you know more clearly what's next on the agenda. Charge the thoughts when the operations are affected. Dig deep in to your core and let all the joy and light appear once again. Nothing can stay under cover for long if it's meant to be used for the source and the light work. Many know that to be true but are still wondering and in doubt at times. Don't think too much about it all. You will be told when the divine time is activated. Today and more tonight will tell the true story and you still can be an observer and study actions and reactions.

Blessings with your work and you're climbing upwards. TttA

ENJOY MOTHER EARTH!

Send out more care and love to mother earth. The planet is greatly distressed because of mining oil and all the pollution. The nature spirit is working overtime to keep all in better balance. When you send out love and light you connect with the forces of nature. It will be an instant reaction and you can stand by and watch how their life force is altered and it will show in their growth. The same goes for people when you light up your lighthouse and send some of us to heal, help and hurry up to help aid a situation. Detach after and cutting off the thread then go to next situation. Stay a bridge worker, healer and teacher. Some will not accept but that' not your problem. Many will only use the spiritual energy to feed on. They should learn to connect to the source themselves. No progress if no homework is being done. Many souls' true feelings are being challenged. Stay with the eternal order and progress will follow.

Blessings and love from us all. TttA

ENERGY EXCHANGE!

Remember all that we have told you about that. If you don't exchange either money or work of the same value the energy goes out to the other person. And that will make a depletion so have another look at that subject The sort out time is to know exactly who is who you don't think sometimes that somebody could be so much controlled and devious now you have seen more. Leave them all to us and cut the connections. Others will come with better motives and to learn about the universal pattern. Still go ahead as we advise you, and leave all judgement to us. We are the only ones that know all their conditions. We have trained you very severely to the very breaking point at times. We have to make sure that you were acting accordingly to the standards we have given you. Work a little more on focusing, other areas are quite good. Let the day unfold as it will. We are still checking your doors and extra guards are supplied.

Blessings and love to all. TttA

EASY DOES IT!

Relax; the interference is not your fault. Something or somebody is around you to make you feel or think so. Detach and cut away all that thought you have enough of work in many areas. Focus on that and let us do the rest. Just before you are going to advance you will get more interruptions. Wait and enjoy something every day as the progress you have made is your progress and let others work on theirs. Let it be if we say so. It's nothing new to be attacked. The higher you go the more severe the attacks. Give that entire situation to us. As we have said the ones that try to deter you will be very sorry they even tried. Most do not know how well connected you are and very few recognise what's going on. It's not too easy as some might think but the only thing you can do is to ignore it. They are only after energy. All those are under negative control when they act as they do. Let us bless you and keep you. Regards to all light workers and companions.

Blessed be. TttA

RUN THE WHOLE RACE!

Let's think about that as many are not doing that. For so long it has been hard work and a lot of learning so they think they have more important experiences that are just too much them and so they give up with the goal in sight.

Think about the waste of not being able to get through. Bide your time when this situation arises it's all fit and all involved are being tested to check what you will do in adverse circumstances. Let things be if and when you do not know what to do. Waiting is hard for some but divine timing comes in to it and it could easily be revived by acting too fast. You know patience is also another part of your development as we have said so many times, but today is just a reminder about keys and how to recognise the events. Let today flow and leave all quarries to a better more focused day. As you have noticed the weather has changed and it's a part of the alterations in the solar system. Be prepared for more of that sort so take the opportunity to use the good times in between for your own work.

Stay calm joyful and remember our wisdom. TttA

USE THE LIGHT WAND!

Use all the viable tools that we suggest to you and know which once and at what time. Practise and keep on practising and you will get the pattern of it all. Let my guiding light help and show you the right book in the universal wisdom. The book will only open when there is a real need and you have enough respect for the knowledge. Don't waste time and take the opportunities and use them wisely. The information could easily be misused in the wrong hands. That's why the book is hidden and available for the ones that have the respect and training. Let the day with peace joy and eternal love to all that is entering your sanctuary. You only have to act when we ask you to deal with it all then your energy level will stabilize. Rest is necessary after a session. If you don't you will be put to sleep by us. Listen in and take notice. You are in the making of a new you and we are around you most of the time until you have gotten the last input for your growth at this point. More later, it's all in chapters.

Love and light TttA

EARLY START!

What a sunrise today! Really it was an early start so that you could experience the early rays of the sun and the awakening of Mother Nature. It was also to show you that a change in time was good. Only a little thought to alter and enliven your spirit mind and heart. Go on today with new fresh input and a new sense of refreshment. The sound of the water and the sounds of the bells will also help you to connect with us. Only one more week until the Christ energy comes down on you. That in turn will spread goodwill and experience and alter peoples thinking. It will also aid our group work and less energy will be used and trying to get through. Anything that helps and uplifts you are tools. Look at them as such. At times people and books act in the same way and even the media can inform you about signs and keys. Keep all of that in mind when we connect and exchange grains of wisdom. SMILE.

Bless you all TttA

LET US BLOW FRESHNESS IN TO YOU!

Today clearness and freshness is only a part of your new life. As we have said many times, when one area gets sorted others will follow. A big turnover is about to occur in the universe and on earth. The same as we said when one planet changes the others will also be in a different place. The same for many star gates they will alter also many have to be closed. That was because of aliens that did not have good intentions, so to protect the earth it was closed. New ones will open and let good energy in and also for some of you that need to visit other dimensions. There are ways to connect but not suitable for some. Stand by and observe what's going on and don't get impatient. You have been ready for quite some time but others are not. Keep occupied in the meantime and carry out our tasks. You all that are working for the light must be responsible and reliable in the best way you know how.

Courage and joy from us all TttA

ORDER!

Discipline and order are two valuable parts of every one's training in the spiritual field and the only way to advance to a higher level. There are many others that think and say different. Yes it's possible for many other solutions but the safest way to the goal is not to take too many side-tracks. It's human but not advisable. All of you that are working on your progress are looking at where the path goes and who is likely to be your companion. That is to follow a good leader. Who are you following? Leadership is a serious business and very responsible. To be a leader takes a lot of understanding focus and obedience. Beware of so called leaders that have other agendas mostly ego-trips or too much income. Then you can use the keys to check and listen to your spirit. How does it feel in this person's nearness? Stand back if not sure and ask us how and when. Your group is now altering again. That is good, new input is coming in and you are finding out who is learning or wants to know. Wait and watch is a good indication. Only a week to go and many will hear and see.

Joy and love from us all. TttA

REMEMBER!

The only way to do that is to go back and remember the wisdom from the old days, so many lives and so much learning. At times it has taken years to understand why and how it's working. One life only is far too short to comprehend the source knowledge and information. Let go of many ideas that have gone, as they are a form of preprograming from well-meaning teachers and aids in many forms. Be still and know that I am God the father and you will know the truth. Many students find it hard to accept so we are giving them a simple version of the whole picture and when that's understood we widen the whole picture a little at a time. When teaching anything, you know that you can't give too much at once as it would not fall in to good ground and get lost. Your thought pattern is of very good value it works very fast and you should use it more. Next weekend will soon come and it will make it better still for you and many other light workers. We are getting closer once again so you can sense us around you. Many blessings with love and laughter.

You're ever understanding teachers TttA

LOVE AND LIGHT TO ALL YOUR PARTS!

The cell structure is a living part of your system so send love light and support with encouragement every day to them. Thanks also are very useful. The cells pick up all your thoughts and act accordingly also cell memories are affecting your life and your wellbeing. That's why we often say love yourself first so treat yourself in a nurturing fashion. If only your health system would understand that many more healers including doctors would cooperate and the result will be miracles. Treat the whole person as one with the spirit in charge. The speed of many would accelerate. The same principle goes for all living things. The life force in all living beings is the main substance in all recovery. The life force comes from God the father. To aid our lives and to make it easier to live on this Earth. Enjoy today and give out compassion love and joy. Yesterday's work was quite complex but in time you will understand why. We will send you conformation about all that.

Blessings and cheer from all your teachers and healers.
TttA

RECHARGE IN NATURE!

All tools are given to you to use and enhance your life's work. Remember to activate some of them. Many tools are used to clean and clear someone's life or deal with negativity of all varied kinds. That's not for you to deal with. You are the middle person that's aiding the source and letting us our work through you. Don't think for a minute that you are alone in your work. Many are there working with you with their special talents and many years of training as well as growth. Last night was different again and we wanted the new connection to be able to work with you so only a few were present. The number does not count only the eagerness to learn with love and light. You have known for a while who will be good students and are willing to give as well as receive. The balance was good others will come next week, and will discover what they missed out on. Healing energy and companionship was extra good. We will stay close this afternoon when you are passing on wisdom and explanations. You have started to see why the events have been occurring and why some people have come to you.

Blessings and light TttA

FRESH WIND IN YOUR SAILS!

Let the storm take its course and after you will experience a new energy. The time has come when you least expected but that how it's work in the universal law. Let today enlighten and cheer invigorate and water your spirit. A fresh spirit is a strong link to us. When you are weary after trying for too long or trying too hard, no good work will come out of it. Rest and go back to your father and after you will come back and do more work for spirit. This weekend will be something to remember. All the work you have put in for the last four years will bear fruit. New connections and new energies are arriving on your door step. Surprise- surprise you did not expect that to happen so soon. Tying up loose ends and sorting out so many areas has taken a while but you did persevere and always will.

When you completely surrender you will get a completely wonderful day. We have not told you of late? Too many details? That was for a reason. All was not clear what, who or when so you are doing exactly what we thought you would. Thank you for your patience.

Joy and wisdom claim miracles. TttA

STILLNESS AFTER THE STORM!

Let the peace and tranquillity enter your soul after all disturbances. The storm stirred up a lot of feelings and past memories. Let it be just that, passing phases of events. Learn from them and remember what appeared when you looked at it. Let the dust settle and enjoy the freshness of sun and water. You felt the force of nature and that will happen more and in many different ways. Stay flexible and take a day at a time as no one knows really when and how. Many have ideas of thought forms and wisdom from so long ago. All of that is fine but remember I am the one that knows and we have given you pictures and information and that's all you need to know for now. Try to leave all others to us. And only do your part. You have had many jobs lately only to practise and make sure you are not overdoing any tasks. Today there will be other revelations. Take every searching soul in to your sanctuary to reconnect them with the source once again.

Enjoy and relax! TttA

WORK AND REST!

Balance is the word for the day. There are so many that do not understand the value of that word. Be an example for our laws and wisdom. You don't have to be perfect, only do the best you can and we will give you the strength to carry on. Your life is about to change again and all the alterations are a part of the transformation after the storm and will sort it out. You need to keep in mind what we have said easy does it. Don't try to hard or do too much at once. Do your daily task with us and all the knowledge is doing you good. A very focused and disciplined life is not for everyone. You have been told that's why we give you severe lessons. Bear with it a little longer it's getting sorted and we want you to relax in between. Claim peace joy and health for every 24 hours. Order and love will get you through. Let today be a day to getting closer to us. We know how you feel for now, that will change so look forward to the new you.

Blessings and love. TttA

A NEW WAY OF LIFE!

After all that reconnecting and rediscovering you need a little time to adjust. Take it as a refreshment time? You all have a lot of thinking and renewing to do and good wisdom and you will do more. Take a day at a time and enjoy a little positive life in between. Balance is still the best way. Today will be a milestone in your life that you have been waiting for a long time. The conditions had to be suitable for all concerned. All will be well and better than you think. Leave the details to us with your rejuvenation. Relax in between jobs and try to see more of what's going on. Nature will help you to recharge and be who you are and were such a long time ago. Don't take too much notice of others that try to ignore you. They have their problem not you. Go on and enjoy a little nurturing today as well as yesterday. We did help you to make the most of it and encourage you to stay patient and calm.

Love and support from all of us. TttA

LET ME DO THE INVIGORATION!

Let us heal and guide you on your path to your goal. Nothing is for nothing so bear with it as it comes. We do know about your thoughts and we are with you all the time. Yesterday was important even if you did not think so at all times. Little by little it will unfold and as we have said one day at a time. Your life is so changeable at present so take it easy and rest when you want to. Go ahead today and we know that you know gathering for the month of November will be gone and all your unease with it. Your own health will follow the pattern. Let the strength and vigour enhance your day to be unfolded as best as it can for now. Stay patient and move slowly and keep close to us. You are having practical help and we have sent that thought to different sources around you to aid and cheer. The weather is now quite pleasant. So enjoy that and all the new flowers with so many different colours.

Joy blessings and wisdom TttA

LIVE AND LET LIVE!

Yesterday is one so learn from it. Keep the wisdom and let the rest go. Hard for many at times to understand and practise. Keep working at it and you will get there. So many questions to answer in a short time. Let's deal with one at a time as that will do it. You also want to teach others and you are. Stay calm and be patient as possible and rest in between work. Beware of thinking that now that is not so. You are still the scribe and connection with earth and heaven. Look at it as a time of learning healing and to activate what's been lying down for so long time. Gathering dust now is the time to spread the knowledge to so many others and to use it for you as well. Today introduction was a great start for the evolvement for the ladyO. She will in time teach others and grow herself into a wonderful soul. Blessings in rich measure for all your work and a lot of encouragement from us all.

Extra blessings TttA

SURRENDER!

My beloved children you did say and you did do the surrendering. Now and then you get impatient and want to know exactly when and how. That's not for you to decide. Listen to what's happening. Mean what you say and let us do the work on you and for you. Too much from your own energy will deplete you and then when tired you can easy get into bad habits. Relax and wait for the result as it will come sooner when you leave all of it to us. You are so eager to move on so a little more patience and trust would be advisable for all concerned. Stay calm and enjoy life's little things that could easier wait to be dealt with. A little at a time will get you there. The same as a brick, one brick after another build a wall. But one brick dropped on you will do the damage. Stay together and encourage and uplift with all your tools. Use them and teach others different skills.

Courage my friend and student TttA

REJOICE!

Try a little more to show joy. So many people are lacking in just that. Trials and tests have come down on very many at this time. All will benefit for times ahead the tests have been hard and very desponding for some. It is always darkest before the dawn. Stay with it and find little things that will enhance your day and others. The wonderful picture of love and beauty in your garden will heal and invigorate all that come and sit for a little while. Some will come back, and others have gotten what they were looking for at that time. That's not for you to think about, as the freshness after the rain will also help. The life-force of all the greeneries and all the varied colours will also do their part. The stillness after the thunder yesterday cleared the air. Keep on surrendering every morning as we are dealing with the situation in the best way possible. It will take a little time but it has been worked on for many years. Take today as it comes and enjoy your garden and the good vibrations.

Courage and love from all of us. TttA

KEEP GOING!

That's the word for today. You all have been tested and tried because of the changing in the whole system in the universe. People like you feel it more strongly so stay clear from disturbing people and news for now. Let our peace and joy enter your mind and body. Go for a walk amongst the flowers and listen to the wind. Wait until the end of the month for all changes to be gone. It's so uneasy now so waiting would be wise. Enjoy the moment and don't try to work out the future. Let's do it together and all areas will be fine in the end. Help is on its way as you have asked for yourself and others. We heard you and all requests will be dealt with. Most people that have come to you have karma to sort out. Forget, forgive and realise is very important. Many don't understand why but it's coming to the surface, situations, events and conditions. One of your old friends from so many lives ago has come to learn and put his life together once again. We are with him for support, guidance and input whatever is needed. Take care and keep going the best way you can. Thank you.

Love light and wisdom. TttA

MEDITATION AND COMMUNION!

Let today be a day of meditation. The beginning of a new week and to strengthen the line to the father. Where from all life comes. To cooperate and live in the unseen part of the time also will benefit you. So much input will guide and help you on your journey towards your goal. You all are on never ending travel through space and time. That is what is all makes it all worthwhile. Many ups and downs will occur but that's life as you say on earth. Forever growing and being wiser with the responsibility. Look at it from another angle. We have told you to do so for many years now, so try again so you are growing others might not follow, leave them to us. We will give them the same changes; it's a matter of free will and understanding the value of every single day, and its events. Life is so complex at times and people make it more so many times. To prepare the ground is our work. Yours to nurture and weed. The big pictures are emerging and stay vigilant.

Blessings and love from us all. TttA

DON'T LET THE LITTLE INTERFERENCES DETER YOU FROM GOING TO BIGGER HEIGHTS!

That is a big wisdom sentence. You know by now that we will increase your wisdom when we think you are ready. At present time so many are confused and unsettled. New energy waves have been coming in to you now for many weeks. And sensitive people will pick up that much more from the environment. Some also get an extra boost of wanting to do more. Others might not understand, but you do. Stay calm and organized and all will be well. The music tonight will bring you many more feelings of peace and tranquillity. This may sound different to some but the level of growth will aid you and help others to heal and discover long lost wisdom once again. Whatever level you are on, you all will benefit from the vibrations. Shakuhachi flute its every good tool for many. Enjoy the music for relaxation healing and peace of mind. We will attend your meeting tonight.

Wisdom and courage from.us. TttA

DEW DROPS AND SUNRISE!

Let the freshness in the morning help you get a start on today's work. Unexpected happening will occur. As we have said when the timing is right it will happen. All that patience and discipline has done its work and now you will see many miracles happen. Last night was another proof of that. All the love and the healing went out to all that were present. They will notice and come back for more. You only have to ask and we come faster than any of your earthly helpers. All in all you needed to see and experience close up how simple it all is. Use your garden for many different purposes you will know how and when. Keep learning listening and smiling your life is changing once again. We do still have it all in hand. The universe is rich so take the latest surprise as an encouragement from us to keep up your work and support others in their quest.

Lots of joy, health and wisdom and light from the whole team. TttA

TRY AGAIN!

Yes you did find that out today, so many times and still not working. Have a break and try later. The heat wave is hitting many parts of your life. Spend time with us and all will soon work again. So many are ready to connect with you, but some are still pondering about when. That's OK and you know that's not your work. We are sorting that out. Watching and working for a little while longer keeps the communication going, never lose the line to us because you need us and we need you. The weather pattern is also altering. Only two more days and the energy pattern will settle down. Wait a little longer and keep on doing your work that wanted attention. Enjoy the solitude for a chance to restore. Spend the rest of the day receiving all you can from us. And keep on delivering to others of your spear energy.

Blessings and love from us all. TttA

CUT AND DETACH!

Today we will have a little talk about how you can keep yourself and your energy guarded and protected. When on the phone for whatever the reason,after stop cut and detach. By doing that you will keep yourself from being influenced by others and some negativity. The same goes for people working in and out of hospitals or similar places.

Stay alert otherwise you could easily pick up negativity from others and unwanted thoughts. We have told you that so many times. But you all need a reminder now and then. Repetition is the way to keep the knowledge from the well of life alive. So much is getting lost if not in order or given time to work and being activated and kept alive. Still be selective and keep your priorities in balance. It's too easy to get side-tracked when to many situations crowd you in. Stay as you are and keep on giving us our set time. Respect most- goes both ways. We all have other actions to take. Let the love and light brighten your path.

Wisdom from TttA

LAST DAY BEFORE IT'S ALL ALTERED!

My beloved children you are following through the best way you know how. It has taken you a while but all learning does. Still we say all in balance and you will get there. The big surrender morning and night is of big value to you all. How else can you get the right help for the individual person? Many live quite a tangled life so more untangling will take longer. In all its lessons to be learned from, many ask why we don't want for that something for that person only to be understood and dealt with. The lesson each life is very specific. So you all need to look into that. Most have preprogramed DNA from so long ago. It runs often in big families and so many other lifetimes together. You have been using your CD disc to alter and enhance your belief and conditions. It might feel harsh at times but you have done it and it has only a little bit to go. Parables were used in old times so the masses could remember the meaning of it all. Do not compare and wonder why and what. It's all in hand.

Love and joy from us all! TttA

TIDY UP AND LOOK WHAT YOU HAVE GOT!

The sort out time is still operating, so keep going as you have started. It might stir up some old energy and you might remember events and signs with actions. Well, have another look at it and keep good memories and get rid of others that are no longer is fitting in to your life as it is now. As you change your likes and dislikes will follow after. It's only a sign of your evolvement. Even what you spend your time on will alter. Its inter woven and followed through from a long chain of connections. You are many times still an observer you will learn a lot from that. Let my light guide you through calm and stormy weather. The whole universe is involved and many actions are still not explained to you, but it's not needed, as your life is a little complex at times but it will get easier after being renewed. Keep holding on to your goal and do rest when tired. Go on with what feels right today. Unfolding times again.

Blessings and healing from us all TttA

IT'S CLEAR ONCE AGAIN!

Today's link in was of a very big value. You have come across a lot of souls lately. Some appear keen or just want to be seen. Well now you know it takes allsorts to work with and understand it all. Today's truth was what you felt for a while as so easily a soul can get tarnished and controlled. Sad story but it is not yours. Leave them to us to deal with. Do only your part. The last tangled case we now have taken in to our care. Thank you for your work and all that energy used for good. The day of happenings is here once again, the whole universal picture is in uproar because of planet changes and other solar systems are also altering. Beware of negative thought patterns and keep an eye on your surroundings. Special skills are now to be used and that's why we have told you to stay calm and peaceful. Love and laughter is also very beneficial. We are dealing with your earthly conditions the fastest way possible. So many troubled souls in a tangled web that many have woven themselves. Love each other and learn a new way of living.

All our love and support. All is well TttA

STEADY AS SHE GOES!

Well now, steady does it. It's not good to rush around in the silly season, as it is named on your planet. Stay calm and enjoy the little good surprises and think about the coming season as a positive event. No one will ever benefit from doing things against your spirit. You will experience something different this time, don't make too many set plans as yet. Spend time apart and connect with your teachers healers and get activated. Then you will have something valuable to bring back to your fellow man. The spiritual interest is getting more noticeable and many are doing what they really wanted for years. That is freedom for all that want to evolve. Let the day unfold in the best way as possible. Some need to take stock of what really is their quest on earth this time. To be able to feel what to do and when is indeed a great gift. Given for all to use not misuse, as some keep doing. Beware of your thoughts this season. Be wise and enjoy.

Blessings and peace from TttA

INSPIRE EACH OTHER!

Stand by in this point in time you would do well to support your fellow man. So much sorrow and grief everywhere. One day later you will think back on this time as a learning and endurance time. Hard for many to hang on and wait but necessary. Life goes in circles and events will occur and come and go. It's not for nothing to be able to accept and remember what comes your way might not be understood at first. Remember how the seasons are changing and they will alter more, yet in the meantime do your work and take time out every day. As we have said many times "don't run on empty". We the source can't tell all the light workers often enough. Back to the inspirations you all will get a refill from us. You only have to ask specifically. Our storehouse is full so remember also to store some in your spirit bank for a time that needs extra supplies. Go on for today as you have started. All areas are being worked on.

Healing wisdom and eternal blessings from us all TttA

LIGHT A LIGHT FOR US!

We all could do with a little more of warmth, love and cheer this season. So many buy and overdo things because it would be expected of them. We have seen so many trying to please or keep the peace every year it goes on and on. We want you to rethink the whole pattern. Spend a little less and put more in your spirit bank and give out love. Light without to aspect anything back. If it comes it will be a bonus. Speak honestly and lovingly to your fellow man. All have different wants and needs so ask them what would warm their soul. Ask us and we will give you good advice. We do know everyone's "make up" and what really helps the person.Beware of trying to impress someone. Give from your heart and do it freely. God always speaks to man but man is not always listening. Too busy or they hear but don't like it so it becomes selective hearing in many cases. Keep up your surrendering and work on your trust.

Blessed be. TttA

SPRINKLE A LITTLE LOVE TO ALL!

Let your love and compassion be with you especially this season. Nurture each other and speak of light and cheer to all. The heat from my sun and the healing and love from my son will help you and empower you all. The Godspark will put the faltering embers once more. Many times it's the ember is the sign of not being connected to the source enough. Never lose the vital line of fresh input that you live off and will grow from. To stay alert and alive is essential. Keep that in mind when you study and to tell others the same. No wisdom will be given if not used or passed on. It would mean stagnation. Knowledge is not meant to stay in the dark or hiding in a dark place. Many of you have been trained to teach, so teach. Old knowledge is fine often misunderstood and many interpretations are too easy to follow check again and again if not sure or feeling uneasy. Water your spirit garden.

Love light and measure from all of us. TttA

UNFOLDING TIMES!

Let you day unfold a little at a time. It's best for all concerned that it is that way. Give yourself time to digest all the feelings energies and alterations. Don't expect others to fully understand what's going on with you. We and you are the only ones that are involved. You will have a few surprises this season of good will. Good feedback is most valuable. One of the best presents you can have. Something coming from the heart and said in honesty teach each other about real love and compassion. No one will get away with lies or deceit anymore. We are doing a big sweep all over the globe. This morning's call was only there to rattle you. We have promised to deal with that case tangled web which was woven in and will take some sorting. Something dark and very negative has taken residence there, to get at you for working to clear. Well now another practise again. Get on with the rest of the day in good faith.

Lovingly yours TttA

CALM AND EASE IN THE CORE OF YOUR SOUL!

Let the calm and peace go in to your very soul. When it has reached the core it will spread out to many other parts of your body. It must come from the inside and go out. The peace and calm comes from the father that knows all, does all and love all. The only thing you have to do is ask what is best for your higher self. Let that truth sink in to your very soul. Think for a little while and ask your father and how when and how. You might do some work with or connect. The blue print is there so ask honestly how to best deal with the situation. Prayers are fine talking to the father meditation is also equally good listening to the father. Go back to the Lords prayer that's starts with Our Father. Do a meditation on just that, it's not always understood, particularly the meaning of it all. Ask for what you don't fully grasp. One step one day at a time does it. Every day has enough of its own focus on little events that make your warm.

Eternal blessings TttA

THE TIDES OF LIFE!

Life's incoming and outgoing is a part of the energy flow. You all have at times looked at that happening. The moon faces and nature are also a big connection. Study and know that's all in hand. The universal forces are operating in good order. Trust and have faith and we are very close by in this year's celebrations. Especially this year when so much will appear on the horizon. Go easy on yourself and do only what comes naturally for you. Don't be too busy or do too much so you can forget why you are here. Healing and joy will be given in full measure, but you still have to ask. After that wait and look for a signs and events. If life looks like a maze at times, stop and pause, and climb up on the highest ground to see where to next. We will give you all support and understanding and help you to get on with your work. Stay steady and calm and all will be well. Smile and rejoice in all adversities.

Courage and cheers TttA

A NEW DAY!

Let it be so, yesterday is gone with all the learning and communication. Every new day gives you a chance to learn, grow and heal. You have been asking a lot lately about all these things. It's coming but because of the changes everywhere it takes time. You also have been asked to dig deeper to be able to better understand your life. As it is altering again and not being told how and why it is a little frustrating. We do know how you feel at times, cut off from everyone and everything. That is for a purpose that would hinder your growth and take a lot of energy that is needed for yourself. Try to do your best to unwind in between and take a little time out, Christmas this year will be different, let it all unfold. What comes is meant to come. Give yourself some time out and digest it all. No rush when important decisions need to be made. We are in a standby mode, keep all in order and give away what we suggest.

Love, care, health and joy are with you for ever. TttA

LET US DO THE CLEARING!

If and when we say let us it is beyond your knowledge. Many things that we have said to do or attend to are on your present development and for you to practise on so you can understand all the different levels of science and technology. You on Earth have many versions of the truth, that is why there is so much confusion around. Don't waste too much energy or money on all the different explanations. Quite often just let it be and ask us. We are the only ones that know every one's heart and grade of trust. Today you have had proof once more of the way we operate. We use humans as a grade of knowledge that we check and have extra teachers to. Not all are qualified and would empty out so we can send information down. This years ending will surprise many, the future can be felt by certain degrees but only a little of the big picture. That is also why you should not tell a story before we let you know what was needed in an action. Beware of negative thoughts now when the time is short. The subtle way of working is shown in their actions.

Wisdom love and health TttA

HELP IS ON ITS WAY!

Always remember to ask for help and don't tell us which one should come to your aid. We are in charge of all that. Leave it with us. Only ask who is in charge of your life. You soon will know by the signs and events. Get ready and love and laugh a little more. Lately you have been challenged a lot, but you felt what was wrong and activated it, so you can do your work for us. Prepare for the New Year and the following days ahead. Many have tried to tell you that is not what's going to happen. WRONG! You do know. Keep your faith going and relax in your garden whenever possible. Live one day at a time and you soon will know the rest. All your small enoying conditions will be taken care of. It will be a great relief. Cell structures and DNA take time to get in to the right place. Be patient and don't try to work out the future. It's unfolding to the best end result for all. Don't overdo anything extra because its Christmas month. Give time to yourself and us and keep the good work up.

Blessings and cheers TttA

CARRY ON AS A LIGHT WORKER!

Please carry on as in these days we all need to do our special kind of work. Don't be discouraged if and when it does not happen that you feel or being told. Divine time is different to your Earth time so keep that in mind when you deal with yourself and other people. Much is going on and so many think they know the solutions or many kinds of answers. Listen in and be cautious you know when you feel OK about something or hear your key word. At times you see a picture that is either crossed out or not. That's one way to get a bead of what's going on. There are many other practical uses. Get yourself working on more "a" words. They were given for many uses in many areas. But go slowly as to take it in all at once would not work. Time is a factor so remember that. Let the meditation heal encourage and aid you and your connections. We will be there also. Keep on trusting and working. Never give up. Rest in between.

Love and light from us all TttA

DON'T BE TOO BUSY!

One day slips by and so will others. Stop that neglect before it becomes too much to deal with. So use the same time in contacting with us. Daily contact at the same time is preferable. This time of the year is more apparent for things needed to be done. Get your priorities in order and have another look at people's behaviour as some get too tired and panic or overdo everything. Stand back and look at the pattern. You are all made different so what will apply to you might not suit others. Keep in mind what the main goal is in your life this time on Earth. Many lessons to be learned and so many issues resolved. You have seen so many giving up so near to the goal. It takes time and effort to reach your destiny mend wherever it is needed. Many souls are hard to get through to because they are so wrapped up in their lives and events that are not explained to them. So many questions from everybody. Stay joyful calm and be wise today.

Blessings TttA

LIGHT A LIGHT FOR A SAD WORLD!

Remember to brighten someone's life today. Ask for ideas and whom you should connect to. We are the ones that know every souls deepest feelings and where they are. That is why we ask you to trust us and find an answer as to who where and when to act. You are a fast receiver now, so empty out and you will receive plenty, you know that to be true so pass it on to others. And they in return can also do so. We know that many have asked questions about our coming closer or new teachers that will assist you. Feel what's good for you and who you can trust. The earth is still in an uproar because of pollution and the misuse of its resources inside the earth. To take anything that cannot be replaced is not advisable. Always replace what you can take from any resources. That is to make sure that next generation will live and survive and so it goes on. To break the spiritual and natures law will have its consequences until all will learn.

Keep going and only rest when tired to regain your strength. TttA

IN THE HEAT OF THE DAY!

When that happens you just have to ride the storm out in the best way possible. Rest and relax and drink plenty of water. The nature is reacting to all the changes in the atmosphere. Let us deal with it and it will soon pass. Remember to claim energy for every day when it's needed like today. Storm in different forms and rain and hail with fluctuating temperatures is also appearing. It's all a part of the change. It will affect people in different ways and some get unexplained ailment "out of the blue". It's only temporary so stay with the thought of peace calm and expectations. It's one of the biggest changes in the universe sense the very beginning. Many from other solar system are also observing what's happening on your planet Earth. Don't make the mistake that you are not involved as a keeper and connection. All living things are interwoven and one links to the other. The symbol of life is simpler than you have been told. God the Father is activating it all after it's been orderly made.

Greetings for the seasons TttA

AT LAST WE MEET AGAIN!

So much happening in so little time. We have been with you all the way but as for writing you have had a hard time putting down the words. As we always have said we have always given you needs and wants in one way or the other. We have sent you different souls for different jobs. That's because the subject is more suitable for what is wanted for now. You have been so much of "topsy-turvy" situations of late so you have been asking why. Naturally it's all got to do with the changing of the Earth further in to the photon belt. The big sort out is still going on and you will hear about more passing's. Their life span was finished and needed for other tasks with us. Do not fret over who or when. That's nothing to do with you. Your task is to do what we request. Every day is a new day so carry out what's your part our work. Take it as a learning curve and growth.

Eternal blessings and courage TttA

LET LIFE FLOW!

Yes my children no stagnation in my kingdom. Inflow and outflow has to operate. People and all living things are affected by the same principles. The law of the universe and spiritual is a very strong combination. Follow through that system and you will grow and understand deeper truth. You can only digest what you are ready for, so when you empty out you will have room for more of our teachings. Complete trust and faith is very necessary for all of that. Discard all other issues first you will get the right order with spirit and then all other areas will be dealt with by us. You only have to do your little part in surrendering to us. Unwind and relax the sooner the better to get all work done in its own good time. The timing is not for you to decide. You only know the little that we want you to know. So stay patient and follow our advice and input. We are sending you many delights for your courage and determination.

Blessings of the season TttA

JOY TO THE WORLD!

Once again I said bring joy to the world by giving them my words. A long time ago I was doing just that and the people did not understand what it was. Always try to think about my message and how different it would have been for coming generations. Well now it's time for another revelation. Time is getting short and the universal picture has starting to alter and will show up as a weather change and a different level of energy and magnetism. Don't make any quick statements and wait until the year is ended. So many changes on earth and heaven. People and animals will all be affected. Stay calm and alert. We will be doing all that's necessary for your comfort. Let my light show you the way and listen in to our advice. Only by emptying out you can receive any news. We know that many are confused and bewildered because of all the alterations. Stay with it and wait for the signs of wisdom.

Always yours TttA

PEACE TO ALL!

Let our peace come in to your heart and clear out all the sadness negativity and grief. So many wounded throughout so many life times. Stayed in the cell memories and got buried, to be able to cope. Later on it did resurface and made the time and space go and come up to the surface. Deal with it as a lesson and let us do the healing. So much was not understood at the time so wrong decisions were made. Now when facing other similar situations you know better. As we have said so many times before be an onlooker and stand back from the situation and you will see what other might have seen in you before. It says, to be on target about life, but so much is going on so wait and handle only one thing at the time. For now you need the wisdom for yourself and others before the big universal changes. Be still and know that I am the father. The father and I are the same.

Blessings TttA

WE ALL WISH YOU A GOOD ENDING OF THE YEAR.

Make the most of it and pay attention to your feelings, energies and weather. We are carefully watching over all light workers especially this year. So many need to have support insight and joy. You are a bridge worker so do just that? It's not what some people think but it's not for them to ponder about. Healing old connections and letting go of others is all for the sort out. That has begun. Leave all the major tasks to us. We will still give you what's right for you. Stay calm and relaxed and joyful as much as possible. It's is disturbances in the air and we are doing all we can to keep you safe and wise. Go ahead and sit outside as much as possible the nature will help to settle things down. Also pay attention to signs and hints. We are keeping you occupied and still. Waiting is not easy for you but you are getting better every day.

Rich blessings to you all TttA

ANOTHER END TO A CHAPTER!

Remember how long a year seems in the beginning and so many memories wisdom you have gain at the end. It's like building a wall of bricks. You do only that in a certain pattern and to make it last you apply the principles of science. It's no good try out something that will not last. That is why curiosity gets so many people to waste time on a project going nowhere. Well now many say what about in versions that are fine. We are given ideas to suitable subjects to pass on to be of use to many for all mankind. Many ideas of ideas come from the negative side so the result is negative. There are two sides to all ideas thoughts and events. Ask yourself where is it coming from also how does it feel. Does it have any ego sides to it or just a temptation? All situations can do for or against humanity? As a bridge worker you have seen it all and you will see more. Stay in our presence and we will support and guide and give you wisdom when or how to act.

Eternal blessings from us all TttA

PREPARATIONS!

To do your home and ground work is of great value once again. You have been asking questions of value so many want to know the answers. We will tell you when you are ready. A different soul needs different levels of explanation.

Otherwise they will not understand at it would help them to connect and understand. Different classes and different speed is going on, so be patient with all that entering your place they have come for a purpose so let us tell you what to say do and think. You wonder how long and how much at times. Well that's a hard question to answer. It's really up to you know what the level of surrendering is. We keep on saying to you to leave it to us. Your life is so complex so it takes planning and activation in a speed suited for you. Your system is so extra ordinary reacting so we can only give you in doses. Because of your nature you are such a strong force, so the attacking has been quite severe. Enough for every 24 hours you know what we mean.

Harmony and joy from TttA

HELP IS ON ITS WAY!

My child of light so many trials and tribulations in a short time. It was necessary for your test. We have to be absolutely sure that you could cope and how much faith you have now. We felt for you in your darkest hour but that was also a test. Only a few more days now and the old earth year has gone never to return. Look ahead and still we say a day at a time. Your physical is being over hauled. And that is not always easy to cope with. In the meantime we are doing all we can to ease the conditions. It's all in hand only for a short time now and you will feel a lot better. Healing is given every day and night. A special team has been assign to you for your welfare. Bear with it and the end result will be very good. You have had so many questions this year. It's now up to you and a more advanced system. Follow through and we are guiding you as always. Prepare yourself and others if they ask for the survival in the best possible way. Don't be alarmed or distressed it's a mind infiltration of the Medias. Stay as you are for now.

Blessings. TttA

RETURN WHAT'S NOT YOURS.

It's a good old way to return and pay up in the end of the year. A fresh start and a clean slate is one of the preparations. Look at each year as a learning curve. Life is there to help you to understand and get more knowledge. You do choose your life where you have a chance of thinking and to learn why how and who. The basic pattern is quite easy when you dig deeper you need to ask what the lesson is for you this time on Earth. You would do well if you let us unfold your blueprint. And then pass on to you what is beneficial for you each cycle. The hardest part for many of you is to stand back and wait. The time is not wasted. Don't look or act in haste. Unfolding takes time. So look in to the surrendering. Most humans are acting on their own instinct and think they know best, without knowing all the information. This day is given a chance to say or do what's needed to mend or make a bridge between spirits. To unite make the unit much stronger. For next year the word is communication. Ask us for the words.

We are closer this year than before. TttA

Printed in the United States
By Bookmasters